The MODERN CHEESEMAKER

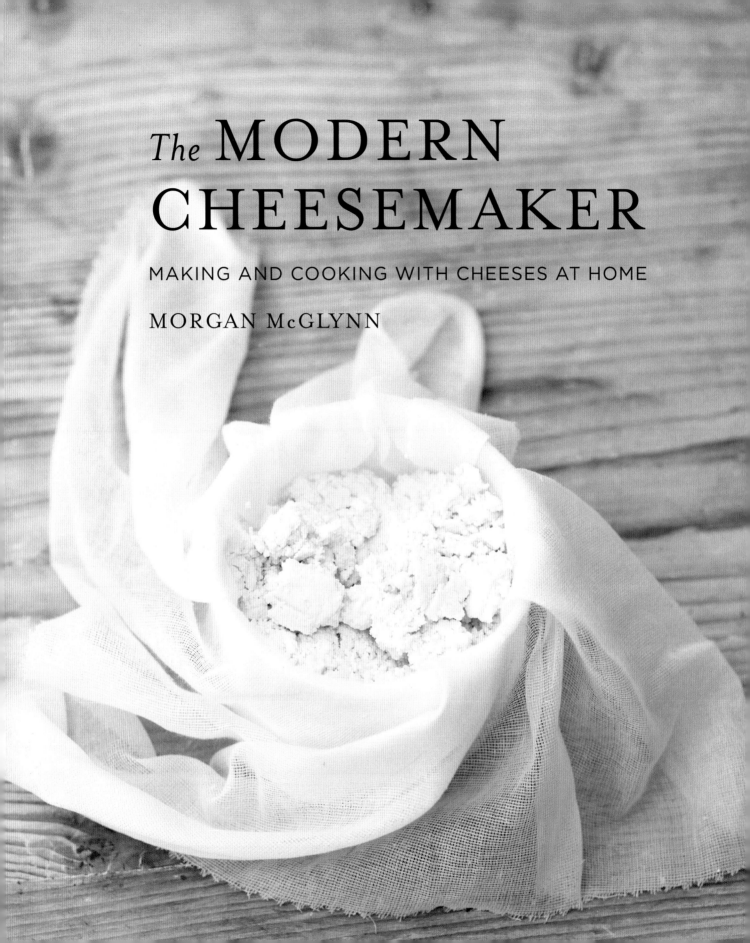

The MODERN CHEESEMAKER

MAKING AND COOKING WITH CHEESES AT HOME

MORGAN McGLYNN

To my Dad, Mum, Bryn, George and Cicely,
I love you so much.

P.S. Thank you for putting up with the smell of
cheese for so long. My heroes!

First published in 2019
A Jacqui Small book for White Lion Publishing,
part of the Quarto Group
The Old Brewery, 6 Blundell Street,
London N7 9BH, United Kingdom
T (0)20 7700 6700 F (0)20 7700 8066
www.QuartoKnows.com

Design and layout copyright © 2019 Jacqui Small/Quarto
Publishing Group
Text copyright © Morgan McGlynn
Original photography copyright © 2019 Jacqui Small/Quarto
Publishing Group

Publisher: Jacqui Small
Design and Art Direction: Maggie Town
Photographer: Jamie Orlando Smith
Editor: Sian Parkhouse
Copy editor: Rachel Malig
Production: Maeve Healy/Robin Boothroyd

2020 2021 2022 2023 /
10 9 8 7 6 5 4 3 2 1
ISBN: 978-1-911-127-87-1

A catalogue record for this book is available
from the British Library.

Printed in China

Contents

6	My Love for Cheese
8	Cheesemaking
11	Cheese Seasons
12	Making Cheese
17	Cheesemaking Equipment
20	The Basic Steps

26 Fresh Cheese
30	Curd Cheese
36	Ricotta
38	Very Indulgent Ricotta
44	Mozzarella
52	Burrata
60	Mascarpone

66 Cream and Soft Cheeses
70	Cream Cheese
74	Cottage Cheese
78	Brie

84 Goat's Cheese
88	Creamy Goat's Cheese
92	Crumbly Goat's Cheese

98 Semi-hard Cheese
102	Paneer
112	Swiss Cheese
120	Halloumi
126	Feta

134 Hard Cheese
138	Cheddar
150	Red Leicester
156	Gouda

174 Blue Cheese
178	Blue Cheese

188 Cheesemonger Tips
190	Flavouring Cheese
202	Accompaniments for Cheese
206	Cheese Pairings
209	Seasonal Cheese Boards
218	Storing Cheese
219	Making the Most of your Cheese
220	Sourcing Ingredients and Equipment
220	Cheeses from Round the World: Morgan's Selection
222	Index
224	Acknowledgements

My Love for Cheese

This is a book for all fellow cheese lovers.

My life has been consumed by cheese, in the best possible way, from my early years visiting my local cheese shop, then going on to own that very shop many years later. Along the way my love of cheese has been kept alive by my travels all over the world, discovering new and exciting cheeses.

I love all cheese – soft, hard, blue, goat's, stinky, creamy, crumbly or mild; there is rarely a day that goes by without me grabbing a bit of cheese and a dribble of honey, crumbling some cheese over a salad or including some in my evening meal.

From a young age my parents would take me to our local cheese shop in Muswell Hill, London, not knowing that one day it would become a major part of my life. As a child I remember the shop sparking a reaction in me – the smells, the feel and taste of all these cheeses I was yet to discover. Each visit was an experience, with new cheeses appearing on a regular basis – new shapes, sizes, colours and smells. I would later learn that this was down to the changing of the seasons, and determined which cheeses would be on offer that Saturday.

A few years later, while studying graphic design at university, I started work as a Saturday girl for the shop, then just two years later, at 21 years of age, I took a huge gamble and bought the shop, cementing my love of all things cheese, so much so that I have dedicated an entire book to the subject.

Since taking over the shop, I have come across hundreds of cheeses in the course of my work, and we now stock over 250 different kinds of cheese, all tasted and handpicked by myself.

Cheesemakers all over the world are producing incredibly delicious, complex and award-winning cheeses, and along my journey I have met some fantastic people. I have picked out a few of my favourite cheesemakers and included their stories and details of their beautiful cheeses in this book.

Over the last couple of years I have also spent time working with some of the most influential cheesemakers, and some of the new trail-blazing urban cheesemakers, who are changing the cheese industry for the better.

But let's not forget that only a few generations ago, people would make their own cheeses at home. It is a real shame that so few of us attempt this now, worried that it is too difficult, too complicated or that you will need lots of equipment. The truth is that you could probably make a cheese with the things you have in your kitchen right now.

I am passionate about rekindling people's love of cheesemaking, and in this book I am thrilled to be able to share my expertise and knowledge

of how to make your own cheeses at home. It is such a rewarding journey, which starts with a simple ingredient, milk, which can be transformed into the most delicious cheese.

I adore handcrafted cheeses and I love making good cheese, but I also love cooking with produce that I have made myself, and I am delighted to pass on a collection of classic mouthwatering recipes, such as Cheese Fondue (see page 165), the ultimate Mac and Cheese (see page 146) and Welsh Rarebit (see page 143), as well as some new and exciting recipe ideas. All the recipes are versatile, too, so you can use your own homemade cheeses or whatever cheeses are available to you.

This is a complete guide to cheesemaking, with easy-to-follow instructions to help you make and cook with the most delicious cheeses at home. Whether you are a curious cheese lover or an experienced hobbyist, this book should satisfy your appetite.

Cheesemaking

I was inspired to start making cheese at home after my job as a cheesemonger took me all over the world, visiting my suppliers and witnessing the ways in which they make their incredible cheeses. Each one uses a different and original technique, some revolutionary, some passed down through many generations.

I love the way this craft was born from something quite simple, to go on to be used all over the world, by so many different people from various walks of life, all united by the act of cheesemaking.

Every culture in the world has its own cheese, all made following a similar principle, which suggests a common ancestry. Even countries such as China, not known for its dairy products, has its own type of cheese, Rushan, an Asian semi-soft cheese, made by the Bai people. And then there is the more unusual queso blanco from South America. Yet it was in Europe that a large variety of cheeses were developed, many of which have become our cheeseboard favourites today.

There are thought to be 3,500 varieties of cheese being produced across the world. And now the trend is entering our homes too, with more and more people having a go at making their own cheese without setting foot on a farm or getting down and dirty to milking a cow.

THE HISTORY OF CHEESEMAKING

The history of cheesemaking is full of fascinating stories, and it dates back around 5,000 years. Originally, cheese was created by a wonderful accident: herdsmen transported milk in leather bottles, and rennet, an enzyme found inside a calf's stomach, would cause the milk to curdle, thus creating the first recorded cheese.

The development of blue cheese was another fantastic accident. One legend has it that a French shepherd left his cheese in a cave while he was in pursuit of a lady, and when he

returned he found the cheese had formed mould. When he tasted it, he discovered it was absolutely delicious. Although this story is a bit fanciful, never the less it has its place in history! The blue mould is abundant in the air and grows rapidly under certain conditions, so the natural blueing of the cheese was a result of the environment it was left in – in this case, a cave.

The features of certain cheeses also give a little insight into our history. For example, at first glance a Valençay cheese (an ash-coated goat's cheese) is a beautiful French goat's cheese. However, it used to be a perfect pyramid shape. When Napoleon returned from a disastrous campaign in Egypt, he stopped at the castle at Valençay, and their local pyramidal cheese apparently aroused such unpleasant memories that it is believed he cut the top off with his sword in fury, leaving the shape that survives to the present day.

So could you be the next one to discover or create a new cheese by accident...?

CHEESEMAKING AT HOME

I have written this book for anyone who would like to make cheese at home for their own use, and learn about the art of cheesemaking. I find making cheese a calming, satisfying exercise, great fun and very therapeutic. And by making cheese at home I have developed a strong appreciation for the effort that goes into all the beautiful cheeses I have been selling in my shop for years. Like many other people, I like to know where my food comes from, and when you make cheese at home you are witnessing every stage of

the process. Homemade cheeses are free from the chemical stabilizers and colourings used in many supermarket cheeses.

As you begin making cheese at home, you will make some good cheese and – inevitably – some not so good cheese, but stick at it and don't be discouraged by less than perfect results. Cheesemaking is a learning curve, and you will experience successes and failures. Yet it is a pursuit filled with endless potential: you can make anything from basic fresh cheeses to shopworthy artisan cheeses.

I have structured the book in such a way that you can progressively build your cheesemaking skills. I started by making the easiest fresh cheeses, and built complexity from there. I found that starting from the beginning and building my skills meant that I was able to progress in small and manageable steps. So if you are a beginner I would encourage you to do the same.

With each cheese you make, you will want to adjust and rework the recipe in your own way as you develop your skills and gain a better understanding of the cheesemaking process.

Cheese Seasons

It is easy to forget that cheese is a product of the land and is therefore seasonal, just like fruit and vegetables. For example, although cows are milked all year round, cheeses made with cow's milk can vary in flavour depending on the quality of the pasture the cows are feeding on.

Certain cheeses come and go as the seasons change, depending on the effects of the weather on the soil and pastures that the animals then graze on. Although most cheeses can be enjoyed throughout the year, some are sublime at particular times and best enjoyed then.

LATE SPRING TO EARLY AUTUMN

I believe that this is the best season for cheese production, as the temperature means the cows and goats are grazing on pastures of flowers and herbs. Most cheeses are at their prime between April and November.

At this time of the year, cows and goats move to higher ground, where the climate is dry and the earth is rich, enabling flowers to grow. These lush pastures result in the animals producing excellent-quality milk, the flavours natural and fruity. This period is when some of my favourite cheeses are produced.

LATE AUTUMN TO EARLY SPRING

The seasonality of cheese can also depend on the animals themselves: some do not cope well with cold winters and are moved inside for shelter. They are fed on a silage-based diet, which does affect the taste of the milk they produce. This isn't to say that these cheeses are not fantastic – two multi-award-winning cheeses, Camembert and Pont L'Évêque, are both produced during the winter months, when the cows are being fed on a maize (corn) diet. These cheeses, justifiably, are firm favourites during the Christmas period all over the world.

Another good example is the king of seasonal cheese, vacherin mont d'or, from Haute-Savoie, an incredibly indulgent runny and soft cheese, with a rich, nutty taste, excellent for fondues. This cheese is only available from September to March, but it really is worth the wait.

CHEESE FROM THE MOUNTAINS

When I think of incredible French cheeses, I think of the artisanal cheeses of the Alps and Pyrenees. These are perfect examples of seasonal cheeses: in the summer the herds move up to the flower-filled fields of the high mountains and eat their fill of fragrant grasses. As soon as the first snow starts to fall, the herds begin to make their way down the mountain, and the milking and cheesemaking processes continues as they descend. When they arrive at lower ground, it is winter and the cows are kept in sheds; the winter cheeses that are produced have a very different flavour. These full, nutty, rich cheeses are still highly sought after.

Making Cheese

Since cheesemaking started around 5,000 years ago, the process has advanced, evolved and refined, but even so it is still based on a simple technique and four very important and essential ingredients: milk, a starter culture, rennet and salt.

Milk is heated, then a starter culture added to acidify the milk. This acts on the milk sugar (lactose), converting it to lactic acid, effectively souring it. Rennet or a vegetarian alternative is then added to this, causing the milk protein to curdle, thus forming cheese curds. Curds are the solids and the whey is the liquid. The next step is to separate the curds from the whey. Once drained, the curds will then be stirred, drained and salted, and finally moulded or pressed to create the cheese. This is the first stage of creating a basic cheese.

The processes you follow in these initial stages of cheesemaking determine the type of cheese that will result – for example, when making soft cheese you would cut the cheese curds lightly and softly, whereas for a hard cheese you would cut the curds finely.

Once the cheese is in its mould, the final stage is ripening, which is when the cheese starts to develop flavour, texture and taste. Again, this is dependent on how and where the cheese is kept, the temperature and humidity – all these elements play a huge part in creating a cheese's characteristics. Subtle changes in the process result in a varied end product.

INGREDIENTS

Cheesemaking, in the most basic terms, is the simple process of separating the milk solids (curd) from the milk water (whey). It requires only a few key ingredients, so the quality of these ingredients is essential to the finished product.

MILK

Milk is the most important ingredient in cheese, whether it's from a cow (the most common), goat, sheep, buffalo, reindeer, moose, or even yak. The methods for making cheese may vary, but cheesemaking will always start with milk.

We often forget that milk is a miracle food, a life-giving substance that contains essential nutrients for infants, whether a human baby or a young calf. Every mammal on earth owes its life to milk. It has all the nourishment needed to sustain life, grow an immune system and bones and provide energy.

Milk contains water, proteins, minerals, lactose, milk fat, vitamins and milk solids. Ideally, you should be using the freshest milk you can get, direct from a good dairy farm, but if you are like me and live in the middle of the city that isn't always possible. Yet if you have a good farmers' market locally, this is perfect, and will give you a chance to talk to the farmers about where their milk comes from, about the animals producing the milk, the way they are kept, and any other advice you may need.

COW'S MILK Cow's milk will probably be the most familiar to you, as it is the most affordable and readily available milk across most of the world. Cow's milk is 88 per cent water, 5% lactose (milk sugar), 3.5–5 per cent protein and 0.3–5 per cent fat, which provides a rich flavour and texture to cheese. The rest is composed of minerals and enzymes.

GOAT'S MILK Goat's milk has become more readily available in recent years, although it is a lot more expensive than other milks. Although it is similar to cow's milk, goat's milk has a lower lactose content, which means it is more easily digested, hence its appeal. It also varies in taste.

SHEEP'S MILK Unlike cow's and goat's milk, sheep's milk is a lot harder to find, and it is very unlikely you will come across it in your local shop. But it can be ordered online or found at larger farmers' markets. Again, sheep's milk is not cheap.

Sheep's milk is high in buttermilk and is a very high-quality milk, which is great for cheesemaking. This milk has a lower lactose content than both cow's and goat's milk, so the health benefits are great.

ACID

The acidification, or souring, of milk is one of the most important steps in cheesemaking. A starter culture is added to milk to change lactose (milk sugar) into lactic acid. (For information on different starter cultures and where to source them see page 220.) This process changes the acidity level of the milk and begins the process of turning milk from a liquid into a solid.

Acid-curdled cheeses, such as cottage cheese, are usually eaten fresh, with the whey drained off and some salt added. They tend to have little flavour because many flavour-producing enzymes do not work well in these acidic conditions.

There are different types of acid you can use, such as lemon juice, which can be found in most kitchens. I use it to make cheeses like paneer. Citric acid is also very easy to get hold of from most pharmacists. It is a weak natural acid that is found in citrus fruits. Vinegar is another natural acid that is used to make cheeses like ricotta and other fresh cheeses. With these natural acid options, you will be limited to making soft cheeses.

RENNET

By contrast, rennet is an enzyme used to coagulate milk. A simple way of looking at it is that before you add the rennet, the milk solids are suspended in water, and they repel each other. But when you add the rennet, the milk solids are now attracted to each other and it does not break them up, allowing them to join together in a much stronger network and form more elastic curds. Cheese made from these curds can be matured for long periods of time, developing complex flavours.

There are several different types of rennet. Animal coagulant is almost always calf rennet, since it is generally accepted that calf rennet produces better-aged cheeses. I would always use an animal rennet, but there are products commonly used as vegetable rennet in home cheesemaking, which are actually microbial rennets made from an enzyme produced by the fermentation of a fungus. While vegetable rennets work as well as animal rennets to coagulate cheese curds, animal rennet is preferred for aged cheeses. After a long ageing period, cheeses made with vegetable rennet may develop an 'off' flavour.

SALT

Cheese salt is a non-iodized salt. Iodized salt can inhibit bacterial growth and possibly slow the ageing process. Cheese salt is available in flakes as well as in grains – the flakes are more easily dissolved and absorbed. But don't panic if you can't get hold of cheese salt: use a good-quality sea salt, rather than non-iodized table salt, because it will be unbleached and will add fewer chemicals to the cheese.

Cheesemaking Equipment

To begin with, I wouldn't advise going crazy and buying enough equipment to start a production line of cheese in your kitchen. In fact, when learning the basics of cheesemaking, you will probably already own most of the items you need.

I have listed the equipment below in order of how essential it is, so to make the easier cheeses you will only need a few of the elements from the list. See page 220 for details of suppliers of cheesemaking equipment.

One of the most important things I have learned since I started making cheese is the importance of cleanliness. Keeping all your equipment spotlessly clean is essential, as unwanted bacteria can get into the cheese and cause odd flavours. I tend to wash all my equipment in boiling water to keep it sterile.

CHEESECLOTH OR MUSLIN You will need this to make all the cheeses in the book. You will use this to drain your cheese, so it must be kept clean. It is a good idea to get a big piece of cloth so you can cut pieces from it when you need them, and different pieces can be used for different cheeses. The cloths should be stored dry, ideally in an airtight container so they don't attract dust. I always soak my cloths in boiling water before using, to sterilize them. This means they are damp when I use them, which isn't essential, but I prefer it as I'm not keen on the feel of dry muslin (cheesecloth).

LARGE SAUCEPAN I tend to use my largest saucepan, which is an old soup pan. A deeper pan helps when the curds are forming, and when cutting the curds, too. My pan has a glass top, so I can keep an eye on the milk when it is souring.

THERMOMETER I use a dairy thermometer, only because it has a long stem and I have quite short arms. But as long as the reading goes from 0–200°C (32–400°F), that's perfect. It is also helpful to find one with a hook to attach it to the side of the saucepan, but this is not essential.

LADLE/SLOTTED SPOON A household strainer ladle will do, as long as the holes are small enough. You can also buy stainless steel ladles specifically for scooping cheese curds, with small holes and a 25cm (10 inch) handle.

CURD KNIFE A curd knife is one of my favourite pieces of equipment, and I think once you explore more cheese recipes this will become an essential bit of your kit. It has a 30cm (12 inch) blade with smooth edges, which cuts through the cheese curds beautifully.

WOODEN SPOON Be sure to get a long-handled wooden spoon that can reach the bottom of the pan. A good wooden spoon is wonderful for stirring cheese: it's comfortable to hold, non-reactive and easy to clean. Stainless steel spoons are another good option.

CHEESE PRESS This helps to apply uniform pressure across a cheese. Some cheeses mature over a period of time, so a cheese press will help to get rid of as much moisture as possible. Most recipes in this book do not require a cheese press – you can use heavy household items such as tin cans or books, or kitchen weights. You can, however, make your own cheese press, and there are plenty of instructions online.

OPPOSITE: **1** Curd knife **2** Cheesecloth or muslin **3** Saucepan
4 Strainer ladle **5** Wooden spoon **6** Dairy thermometer **7** Slotted spoon

OPPOSITE: Plastic cheese moulds in assorted shapes and sizes, and a plastic drying mat.

LEFT:

1 Cheese grater

2 Assorted cheese knives

3 Hard cheese slicer/plane

4 Hard cheese scoop

5 Hard cheese iron (maturity tester)

6 Soft cheese knife

7 Wooden cheese board

CHEESE MOULDS Moulds are used to form and consolidate curds, giving a finished cheese its desired shape. They come in all shapes and sizes, and should indicate which cheeses they work best with, so look out for this information when you are buying them.

OTHER USEFUL CHEESEMAKING ITEMS

- Sushi mats – great drying mats, allowing a flow of air to the cheese
- Colander or strainer – for draining cheeses
- Cheese paper – you can also use greaseproof (wax) paper to wrap finished cheese
- Wire cooling rack – ideal for draining cheeses
- Cheese wax – for waxing cheeses such as Cheddar and Gouda
- Measuring spoons
- Measuring jug (large measuring cup)

SERVING CHEESE

Over the years I have gathered a huge collection of different cheese tools. You can use any knife to cut cheese, but it's always satisfying to use a specially designed tool. These are some of my favourites:

- A cheese slicer (also called a cheese plane) allows you to get more taste from your favourite cheese. Similar to a vegetable grater, a plane is used to shave very thin pieces of cheese from a block.
- A soft cheese knife – the offset thin blade makes it easier to cut through soft cheese such as Brie without pushing the paste out of the crust.
- The fantastic Stilton scoop – a traditional way to consume Stilton is to take a large block and use the scoop instead of a knife. Start in the centre and scoop some out for a wonderful taste of the paste.

The Basic Steps

As we have seen, cheesemaking is pretty simple: essentially, the process is the separation of the curds from the whey, so the solid from the liquid. The transformation of milk into cheese is one of the most extraordinary of all human discoveries. It may sound complicated, but in fact it is a fairly simple and easy process. Making cheese at home can be great fun – you will definitely make good cheese, and you may even make some very good cheese!

1. START WITH MILK

Before you start cheesemaking, it is important to know that the key to a delicious cheese is the quality of the milk. I would always try and find a raw, unpasteurized milk from your local farmers' market, farm shop or specialist deli. Ultra-pasteurized or ultra-high temperature (UHT) milks will not form proper curds for cheesemaking as they can contain additives that inhibit proper coagulation and curd development. Raw, unpasteurized milk is very flavourful and rich, which will result in a great and complex cheese. If that's not possible, use whole organic milk, the fresher the milk, the better. I would buy it and use it on the same day, if you can. Use milk straight from the refrigerator, transfer it to a large pan and begin to heat slowly. When warming the milk to a certain temperature, you are creating the perfect environment to activate the soon-to-be-added starter cultures.

2. ACIDIFY THE MILK

There are many ways to acidify your milk, whether by adding a natural acid like lemon juice, vinegar or citric acid, or a culture or live bacteria. Either way, given time, heat and lack of competitor bacteria, these cultures will acidify (transform the lactose in the milk to lactic acid).

3. HEAT THE MILK

The recipes will vary in temperature and timing, but a good rule of thumb I stick to is to heat the milk slowly; it is not a race, so take your time. The way in which you heat the milk will influence the quality of the cheese you produce. So it is important to keep an eye on the temperature of the milk. You do not want it to overheat, so be sure to remove it from the heat if you see this happening.

4. ADD THE RENNET

Rennet is the enzyme that causes the proteins in milk to link together rather than repel. Adding rennet to the milk will cause it to coagulate and turn to a gel.

5. TEST THE 'GEL-NESS'

When the rennet has had enough time to work on the proteins in the milk, the milk will have transformed from a liquid to a gel. You can test its 'gel-ness' by pressing (with a clean hand) onto the surface of the milk. You should have a big wobbly block of jelly-like curd.

6. CUT THE CURD

What you have to do now is cut the curds into small blocks. You can do this with a curd knife or a long flat knife. The way you cut the curd will affect the amount of moisture that will remain in the final cheese: the smaller the pieces, the drier the cheese will be, and more suitable for ageing.

7

8

7. COOK AND WASH THE CURD

Dependent on the type of cheese, next you should stir the curds, if necessary over a low heat. This is important as the acids are still developing. The more the cheese is cooked, and the more you stir the curds, the drier the cheese will be. Lastly, washing the curds by adding water will get rid of any excess whey. The water will create a milder, sweeter-tasting cheese.

8. DRAIN THE CURDS

Now it's time to separate the curds from the whey. You could do this by simply transferring the contents of the pan into a sieve (fine-mesh strainer) in a sink and leaving to drain. The way that I do it is to line a strainer with cheesecloth or muslin, and place it over a large bowl.

9. GATHER UP THE CLOTH

Next, gather the four corners of the cloth and
bring them together. Try to do this quickly
because you want to keep the heat in the curds,
encouraging them to mash back together to
form a nice smooth wheel. If you wait too long,
the curds get cold and the cheese falls apart.

10. SQUEEZE OUT THE WHEY

Once you have created the bag, all you need to
do is gently squeeze the top to allow the whey to
drain away from the curds. You don't need to use
a lot of pressure, just enough so you see liquid
leaving the bag.

11

12

11. TIE THE CLOTH IN A KNOT

Next, close the bag. Tie up the corners of
the cloth if you can do a simple secure knot,
or just use a short length of kitchen string.

12. HANG THE CURDS OUT TO DRY

Now grab a wooden spoon or use the kitchen tap
(faucet). Suspend the bag from the spoon or tap
(faucet) and leave it to drip above a bowl or sink
for a couple of hours, or however long the recipe
specifies. This will allow the whey to drain off
slowly and completely.

Fresh Cheese

Fresh Cheese

Fresh cheese is a great starting point for cheesemaking; it is the easiest to produce and great to experiment with. I love fresh cheese and make a lot of it at home, as the process is so quick, and you can make most of the cheeses with ingredients you already have in the kitchen.

Fresh cheese is the youngest, purest cheese. This variety is widely popular because it is so simple and has a lovely mild, salty and tangy taste. Fresh cheese doesn't typically have a rind as it is not aged for long periods of time. The texture can range from very soft and spreadable to more crumbly.

This cheesemaking process is very simple: the milk is ripened by adding a starter culture that changes the milk sugar (lactose) into lactic acid, causing the milk to thicken. At this point rennet can also be added to create thicker curds, if desired. Once curds form, the whey is drained away and what remains is turned into cheese. It is that easy!

A lot of people are put off the idea of making cheese at home by the thought of having to buy special equipment and supplies, but these fresh cheese recipes are really easy and require no special tools other than those you would find in an ordinary kitchen. Cheeses like ricotta or goat's cheese can be made using lemon juice or vinegar.

Mozzarella (left) is a wonderful fresh Italian cheese loved by many. A whopping 20 million tonnes (metric tons) of cheese are produced worldwide each year and production is increasing with growing demand.

Délice de Bourgogne (right) is a decadent triple-cream French cheese. Rich and full-flavoured, it has a smooth, velvety, melt-in-the-mouth texture.

Labneh (front) is a marinated fresh yoghurt cheese popular in the Middle East.

Curd Cheese

Curd cheese is a real favourite of mine, beautifully fresh and the simplest of all cheeses, so a great one to start with. Curd cheese is the first stop on your cheesemaking adventure before you move on to some more (ever so slightly) complex cheesy creations. You can also make it a little richer and more indulgent by adding a touch of cream.

2 litres (3½ pints/8½ cups) milk

pinch of salt

2 tsp liquid rennet

MAKES 250g (9oz)

You will need: a cheesecloth or muslin sheet and an instant-read thermometer

1 Put the milk and salt into a large saucepan.

2 Heat the milk to 38°C (100°F).

3 Remove from the heat and add the rennet. Stir in well, until it is completely dissolved, and set aside uncovered for 15 minutes. After 15 minutes, the whey and curd should have separated: the curd will be at the top and the whey at the bottom of the pan.

4 Place your cheesecloth or muslin over a small bowl and use a strainer ladle to gently scoop up the curds and place them into the cloth. Following the steps on pages 24–25, create a cloth bag and hang it over a sink or bowl for about 3 hours to allow the whey to drain off.

5 Remove the cheese from the cloth and it is ready to serve. The cheese can be kept in a sealed container in the refrigerator for up to 1 week.

STAR CHEESEMAKER
BLACKWOODS CHEESE COMPANY, UK

Cheeses: William Heaps, Cow's Curd

The wonderful David Holton and Tim Jarvis started producing the most delicious soft raw cow's milk cheeses in this small dairy in Brockley, south-east London in 2013. They are known for the sensational Graceburn, which is named after a river in Holton's home town. A raw cow's milk feta-style cheese, it is marinated in olive and rapeseed oils with peppercorns, thyme and garlic. They have since gone on to produce four award-winning cheeses, one of which is the Edmund Tew, named after a man who was convicted of stealing cheese in 1829 and sentenced to seven years in Australia.

Curd Cheese Dip

Easy to prepare ahead for a picnic or party, and a great little snack in summer – low in calories, guilt-free and yummy.

250g (9oz) curd cheese (see page 30)
20g (¾oz) chopped shallots
20g (¾oz) fresh parsley, chopped
1 garlic clove, finely chopped
handful of fresh chives, chopped
1 tsp Dijon mustard
1 tbsp red wine vinegar
1 tbsp extra-virgin olive oil
100ml (3½ fl oz/scant ½ cup) whipping cream, lightly whipped
salt and freshly ground black pepper

SERVES 4

Place the curd cheese into a bowl and add the shallots, parsley, garlic and chives, reserving a few chives. Add the mustard, vinegar and olive oil and mix to incorporate everything together.

Stir through the lightly whipped cream and season with salt and pepper.

Sprinkle the remaining chives on top and eat immediately, or cover and chill until you are ready to serve, with some crispbreads and vegetable crudités for dipping.

Ricotta

Making ricotta at home is such a lovely, easy process, and the end result is so delicious, you won't bother buying the stuff in a tub again. It really is as simple as fresh milk, vinegar and about 45 minutes out of your day, and you have produced your very own fresh, creamy ricotta. Homemade ricotta really does have a better texture and flavour than anything I've bought in a supermarket. I love that you can control just how wet or dry the ricotta is simply by how long you let it drain for.

2.25 litres (4 pints/9½ cups) milk
2½ tbsp good-quality white wine vinegar
salt

MAKES 250g (9oz)

You will need: a cheesecloth or muslin sheet and an instant-read thermometer

1 Put the milk into a large saucepan, add a couple of pinches of salt, then place the pan over a medium heat. Keep an eye on the milk and stir occasionally to prevent it sticking or burning. When the milk is almost coming to the boil, you will see small bubbles begin to appear. Remove from the heat when the temperature reaches 85°C (185°F).

2 Add the vinegar and stir gently. You should start to see the curds form. Continue to stir for a few minutes, then cover with a clean tea (dish) towel and set aside for a few hours.

3 Once the ricotta has had time to rest, line a colander with a large piece of cheesecloth or muslin and place over a mixing bowl. Slowly spoon the curds into the cloth and leave to drain for about 1 hour.

4 After an hour, check if the cheese is ready by gently lifting the cloth and squeezing tightly, making sure all the whey has drained out.

5 The ricotta is now ready to eat. It can be stored in a sealed container in the refrigerator for up to 1 week.

1

3

4

5

Very Indulgent Ricotta

The recipe on page 36 shows how incredibly simple it is to make fresh ricotta at home using milk alone. But if you want to make a naughtier version, this recipe, which uses cream and milk, is for you. The ricotta is so amazing that I can simply eat it with bread.

2 tbsp citric acid

8 litres (14 pints/34 cups) milk

pinch of salt

2 tbsp double (heavy) cream

MAKES 250g (9oz)

You will need: a cheesecloth or muslin sheet, an instant-read thermometer and ricotta moulds

1 Dissolve the citric acid in 50ml (1¾fl oz) cooled boiled water.

2 Put the milk in a large saucepan, add the citric acid mixture and salt, and mix thoroughly.

3 Place the pan over a low heat until it reaches a temperature of 82°C (180°F). Stir often to stop it sticking to the base of the pan; heating the milk too fast can also affect the flavour. As the milk heats, you should be able to see the curds separating from the whey. The curds will be solid and the whey a yellow milk substance. Once the milk has reached the required temperature, remove from the heat, cover with the pan lid and set aside for 20 minutes.

4 While the curds are resting, line a colander with cheesecloth or muslin and place over a mixing bowl. Transfer the curds to the colander and leave the whey to drain for about 30 minutes. Add the cream to the curds and stir to combine. Using a slotted spoon, scoop the curds carefully into your ricotta moulds, making sure any remaining whey has drained off.

5 Press down firmly then put the ricotta moulds in the refrigerator to chill for at least 1 hour. Turn it out of the mould and serve immediately to enjoy it at its freshest, or store in a sealed container in the refrigerator for up to 1 week.

Homemade Gnocchi with Ricotta and Basil Pesto

Once you have made your wonderful homemade ricotta, I love to use it in fresh pesto, which I serve with gnocchi. This gorgeous dish is so fresh, and I love how every element of it is made from scratch. This is perfect comfort food.

Homemade gnocchi

4 large potatoes, peeled

2 tbsp butter

1 egg

200g (7oz) plain (all-purpose) flour, plus extra for dusting

salt and freshly ground black pepper

Ricotta and basil pesto

3 handfuls of fresh basil

1 tbsp pine nuts, plus extra for sprinkling

3 garlic cloves, halved

2 tbsp lemon juice

70g (2½oz) ricotta (see page 36)

SERVES 4

To make the gnocchi, place the potatoes in a large pan of cold salted water. Bring the water to the boil and cook for 20 minutes until the potatoes are soft. Drain the potatoes and leave to cool until you can touch them.

In a large bowl, use a potato masher or fork to mash the potatoes with the butter until there are no more lumps. Then add a teaspoon each of salt and pepper and give it a good mix.

Next, make a little well in the middle of the bowl and add your egg. Beat the egg, then use your hands to mix the potatoes and egg together into a ball.

Place the mixture on a lightly floured surface, then add all the flour to the mix. Work quite quickly to knead the flour into the mix until it is no longer sticky.

Separate the mixture into eight, then roll each one into a long, skinny sausage shape about 2.5cm (1 inch) wide. Cut the sausages into 1cm (½-inch) pieces and press lightly with a fork.

Place your fresh gnocchi into a large pan of salted boiling water and boil until they float to the top – usually about 30 seconds – then drain and set aside.

To make the ricotta and basil pesto, place the basil, pine nuts, garlic and lemon juice in a food processor, and process until finely chopped. Add the ricotta and season with salt and pepper. Process again until just combined. Stir through the gnocchi, sprinkle a few pine nuts over the top and serve immediately.

You can also serve the pesto tossed through hot pasta, with grilled chicken or as a dip.

STAR CHEESEMAKER
QUATTRO PORTONI, ITALY

Cheeses: Mozzarella, Ricotta di Bufala

In the hilly landscape of Parco del Serio, Bergamo, you can find the buffalo farm of Quattro Portoni, founded in 1968 thanks to Renato Gritti, father of the current owners Bruno and Alfio. The dairy's mozzarella and fresh ricotta is well known worldwide, but the family has not stopped there. Over the last 50 years they have created a small range of modern buffalo cheeses inspired by their traditional cousins. Quattro Portoni now produces 13 varieties of cheese, all made from their own Mediterranean buffaloes.

Lemon and Raspberry Ricotta Cheesecake

Fresh ricotta is perfect for sweet dishes. This easy cheesecake recipe is an ideal summer dessert.

220g (7¾oz) digestive biscuits (graham crackers)

100g (3½oz) butter, melted

250g (9oz) ricotta (see page 36)

600g (1lb 5oz) cream cheese (see page 70)

4 eggs

200g (7oz) caster (superfine) sugar

grated zest of 5 unwaxed lemons, plus juice of 3 lemons

150g (5oz) raspberries

SERVES 4

Preheat the oven to 170°C (325°F/Gas Mark 3). In a food processor, whizz the biscuits and melted butter until they resemble breadcrumbs. If you don't have a food processor you can crush the biscuits and mix them with the butter by hand. Press the mixture into the bottom of a 23cm (9 inch) cake tin (pan), then chill in the refrigerator while you make the cheesecake mix.

In a large bowl, mix together the ricotta, cream cheese, eggs, sugar and the zest and juice of the lemons. Mix until smooth, then pour over the biscuit base. Chill in the refrigerator for 3 hours until set. Turn out onto a plate and top with the raspberries.

Mozzarella

Understanding how to make your own mozzarella is a fantastic thing – knowing that at any moment, should you desire it, you could whip up your very own ball of creamy cheese, still warm from the whey whence it came. Mozzarella is a really fun cheese to make – there is lots of pulling and shaping, so it's great to make with the kids. Once you have mastered the curd, you can keep this in the refrigerator and make mozzarella quickly and easily whenever you fancy it.

¼ vegetable rennet tablet

1½ tsp citric acid

4.5 litres (8 pints/ 19 cups) milk

1 tsp salt, plus salt for brining

MAKES 2 x 100g (3½oz) balls

You will need: an instant-read thermometer and a curd knife

1 In a measuring jug (cup), dissolve the rennet tablet in 50ml (1¾fl oz) cooled boiled water, stirring until completely dissolved.

2 In a separate jug, repeat the process with the citric acid.

3 Put the milk in a saucepan and add the citric acid mixture, making sure you combine them thoroughly. Gently heat the milk, keeping a close eye on the temperature, and once it reaches 35°C (95°F) slowly add the rennet mixture and stir for 1 minute. Remove from the heat, put a lid on the pan and leave for 25 minutes.

4 After 25 minutes, the curds should have separated from the whey. You can check this by inserting a knife and seeing if it comes out clean, rather like checking a cake. Cut your curds into 2.5cm (1-inch) cubes using a curd knife.

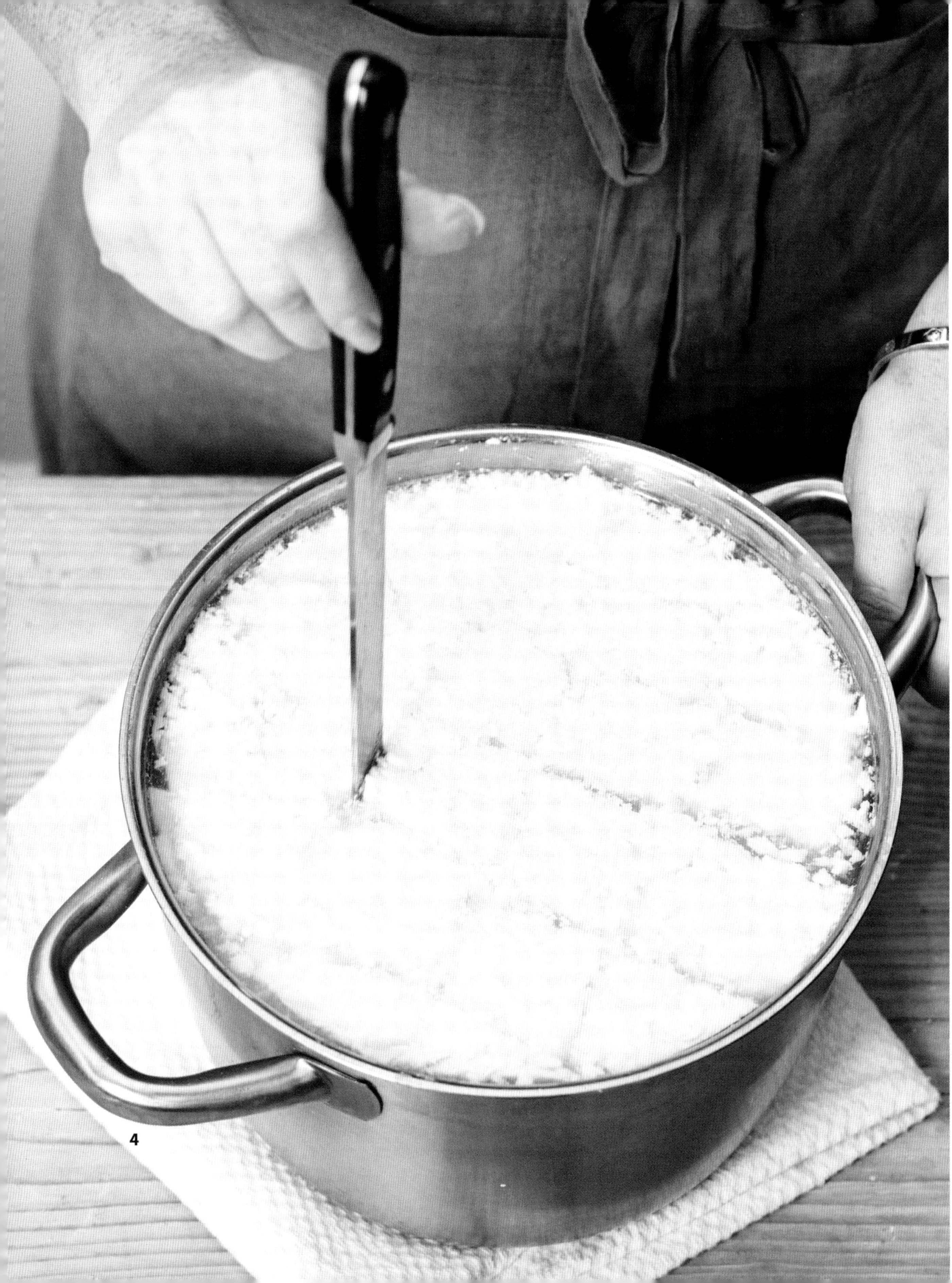

4

5 Add some boiling water to the pan very carefully, not directly on top the curds. Check the internal heat of the curds. It should be around 57°C (135°F). If necessary add more hot water.

6 Using a wooden spoon begin to gently fold the curds, stretching as you fold. If the curds get cool, return them to the hot water for 20 seconds then continue.

7 Repeat folding until the curds become smooth and elastic. Start to work them by hand, wearing gloves.

8 Fill a separate bowl with salted water, ready for the finished cheese. Thoroughly dissolve the salt into room-temperature water (around 700g/1lb 8½oz salt to 4.5 litres/8 pints/19 cups water), then chill it until ready to use. Brine should generally be around 13°C (55°F).

9 Add 1 teaspoon of salt to the cheese, and stretch and fold it for a further 30 seconds. The longer you stretch and fold the cheese, the firmer it will become.

9

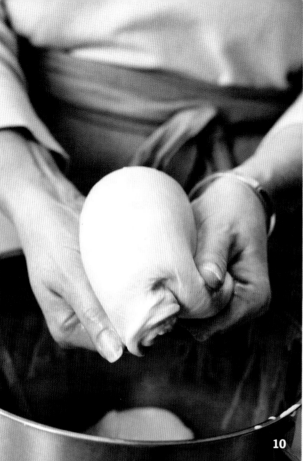

10

10

11

10 Continue to stretch and fold until the cheese has a stringy and shiny texture. Once the cheese is smooth, shape it into a ball.

11 Divide the cheese into two balls. Add them to the prepared saltwater bath, to help with the smoothness. After 20 minutes in the water, the cheese will be ready to eat. Or you can store it, in the salt water, in the refrigerator for up to 1 week.

Baked Mozzarella, Artichoke and Spinach Dip

This super-easy, cheesy spinach and artichoke dip is perfect with toasted baguette slices, crackers or just scooped with a spoon. This is a recipe an American friend made for me years ago, and ever since it's been my go-to recipe for our New Year's Eve party, cosy nights in or if I fancy some delicious comfort food after a long day in the cheese shop.

butter, for greasing

350g (12½oz) grated mozzarella (see page 44)

2 garlic cloves, crushed

200g (7oz) Parmesan, grated

2 tsp salt

400–500g (14oz–1lb 1¾oz) spinach, cooked and drained

200–250g (7–9oz) marinated artichokes from a jar, drained and chopped

100ml (3½ fl oz/scant ½ cup) double (heavy) cream

100ml (3½ fl oz/scant ½ cup) soured (sour) cream

SERVES 6

Preheat the oven to 190°C (375°F/Gas Mark 5) and grease a 25cm (10-inch) round baking dish.

Add all the ingredients to a large mixing bowl, then mix until fully combined.

Pour the mixture into the greased dish and bake for about 25 minutes, until browned and bubbly. Leave to cool, then serve with toasted slices of French bread and dip away!

Burrata

Burrata was first produced in southern Italy, and was created by the mozzarella cheesemakers as a way of using up some of their mozzarella scraps. They would blend them with fresh cream and wrap them up in a fresh ball of mozzarella. Burrata is now a wonderful delicacy in its own right.

homemade mozzarella (see step 1)

120ml (½ cup) double (heavy) cream; more as needed

2 tsp salt, plus extra for brining

MAKES 2 x 100g (3½oz) balls

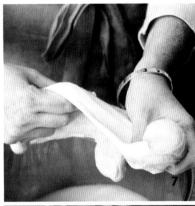

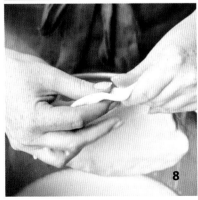

1 Follow the recipe for mozzarella on pages 44–49 to the end of step 4.

2 Now move a quarter of the curds to a small bowl. Add the cream and 1 teaspoon of salt and combine the mixture with your fingers. Set aside.

3 Fill a large bowl with cold water and ice and set it aside.

4 Add 1 teaspoon of salt into the pan of curds using your fingers.

5 Pour boiling water carefully into the pan of curds – not directly onto the curds, but around them until they are submerged. Let them sit for a minute or two.

6 Next, give the cream mix a stir and add a little more cream if it appears too dry.

7 With your hands, preferably wearing gloves (remember, this water is really hot!), shape half of the curds into a ball, then pull and stretch it between your hands, returning it to the water to add heat if needed. Continue to stretch it until it is shiny and elastic. The curds should be easy to stretch at this point. If the water gets too cool, add more hot water.

8 Working quickly, shape the ball into a disc, about 15cm (6 inches) in diameter and 5mm (¼ inch) thick.

9 Place the disc in the palm of your hand and carefully add half the cream mix in the centre of the disc.

9

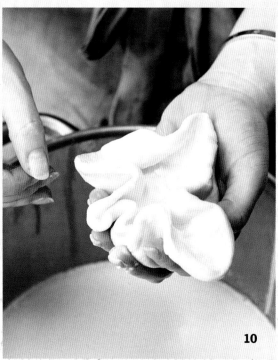

10 Gather the edges together to create a ball.

11 Pinch the top and twist to seal. Repeat with the rest of the curds and cream mix to make a second ball.

12 Place the burrata balls into the iced water and leave for 45 minutes to stiffen up before serving. Or you can store them in salt water (see page 46), in the refrigerator for up to 1 week.

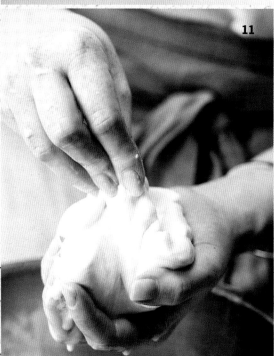

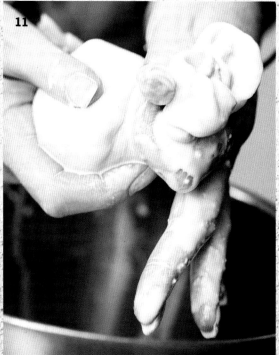

Burrata and Tomato Salad

This salad is so simple, and its success relies on using the ripest tomatoes and beautiful homemade burrata. Choose the tastiest varieties of tomato you can find – sun-ripened, juicy and fleshy – they are perfect for salads! I would recommend making this salad the day you make your cheese, as it such a vibrant, fresh dish.

350g (12½oz) mixed tomatoes (choose about 3 different colours and sizes), halved or thickly sliced

2 pinches of sea salt

large pinch of freshly ground black pepper

pinch of caster (superfine) sugar

3 tbsp extra-virgin olive oil

finely grated zest of 1 unwaxed lemon, plus 1 tbsp of juice

20g (¾oz) fresh oregano, roughly chopped

20g (¾oz) fresh flat-leaf parsley, roughly chopped

small garlic clove, crushed

200g (7oz) burrata (see page 52)

SERVES 2

Place the tomatoes randomly in shallow bowls. Sprinkle with the salt, pepper and sugar, then cover and leave to marinate at room temperature for 20–30 minutes.

Meanwhile, mix the olive oil with the lemon zest and juice. Add the oregano and parsley to the dressing with the garlic and stir to combine. The tomatoes are already well seasoned, so you shouldn't need to add any further salt and pepper to the dressing.

Drain the burrata and place in the centre of the tomatoes. Cut into the top of the cheese with a sharp knife and pinch the sides with thumbs and forefingers to open it up. Drizzle the dressing over the salad, sprinkle with extra pepper if desired, then serve immediately with some crusty bread.

Burrata and Lemon Penne

This is for Friday nights in – the TV is on and I'm in my PJs eating a big bowl of this amazing pasta. Don't be shy with the burrata – more is more. It takes only 15 minutes to make this simple, flavourful and satisfying dish.

200g (7oz) dried penne pasta

2 tbsp olive oil

grated zest of 1 lemon, plus 1 tsp lemon juice

2 garlic cloves, crushed

2 egg yolks

200g (7oz) burrata (see page 52)

50g (1¾oz) pine nuts

50g (1¾oz) rocket (arugula)

salt

SERVES 2

Bring a large pan of salted water to the boil, then add the penne and lower the heat to a simmer. Cook the pasta for about 8 minutes, until al dente.

In a bowl, mix together the olive oil, lemon zest and juice, garlic and egg yolks.

Drain the cooked pasta and return to the pan, then add the sauce, reduce the heat and leave to cook for a few minutes.

Tear your burrata into bite-sized pieces. Add the burrata, pine nuts and rocket (arugula) to the pasta and serve.

STAR CHEESEMAKER
CASA MADAIO, ITALY

Cheeses: Burrata, Mozzarella

Casa Madaio, owned by the Madaio family, is an acclaimed cheesemaker and affineur, located in Salerno, Italy. Through four generations, the techniques of ripening and producing cheese have been handed down from father to son. As reflected in the company's logo, the family home is a castle with three towers. Mr Madaio, the head of the family, said that, to him, the towers symbolize his three children: Angelo, Renata and David, and the future of Casa Madaio. Casa Madaio uses fresh milk – goat, sheep, cow and buffalo milk – as the main ingredient of its masterpieces, such as the superb buffalo mozzarella and burrata.

Mascarpone

Making mascarpone from scratch is ridiculously easy, and only requires two ingredients, so you can quickly whip up a batch of your own fresh and creamy cheese at home the Italian way. Homemade mascarpone has the most beautiful texture – far superior to shop-bought – and is perfect for so many sweet and savoury dishes.

½ tsp citric acid

1 litre (1¾ pints/14 cups) double (heavy) cream

MAKES 300g (10½ oz)

You will need: a cheesecloth or muslin sheet and an instant-read thermometer

1 Dissolve the citric acid in 2 tablespoons of cooled boiled water, stirring until completely dissolved.

2 Pour the cream into a pan and place over a medium heat until it reaches 85°C (185°F). Make sure you keep stirring so the cream doesn't stick to the bottom of the pan and burn.

3 Add the citric acid mixture and stir in. Keep the cream at 85°C (185°F) for 1 minute, then remove from the heat and place the lid on the pan for 5 minutes. Leave the pan on the hob (stovetop) to keep warm, and keep the heat at 85°C (185°F); if you see it dropping, turn the heat to low to maintain the temperature, making sure to stir.

4 Transfer to a bowl and leave the mixture to cool for a few hours or overnight.

5 Set a colander in a large bowl and line it with the cheesecloth or muslin. Pour in the cream.

5

6 Drain the excess liquid off the cheese and squeeze gently in the cloth. Carefully transfer the cheese from the cloth into a bowl. You can serve it right away or it can be kept covered in the refrigerator for up to 1 week.

Mascarpone Chocolate Pots with Homemade Honeycomb

I love Crunchie chocolate bars, and this is my homage to that delicious treat. Making honeycomb at home is so much easier than you might imagine – and everyone loves it, so these super-easy chocolate pots are real crowd-pleasers.

150g (5oz) milk chocolate, broken into pieces

284ml (10 fl oz/1½ cups) double (heavy) cream

250g (9oz) mascarpone (see page 60)

Homemade honeycomb

150g (5oz) granulated sugar

25g (scant 1oz) honey

60ml (2 fl oz/¼ cup) golden (light corn) syrup

1 tsp bicarbonate of soda (baking soda)

SERVES 4

Line a shallow baking dish with greaseproof (wax) paper.

For the honeycomb, combine the sugar, honey, syrup and 1 tbsp of water in a saucepan over a medium heat, stirring until you see the sugar dissolve. Keep an eye on it as it simmers, stirring gently all the time. Continue stirring until the mixture forms a caramel, turning a golden brown colour like warm honey.

Remove from the heat and have the lined dish ready, as the next step will happen quickly.

Add the bicarbonate of soda (baking soda). The mixture will start to froth, so pour it immediately into the lined dish, then set aside for about 15 minutes, or until cool to touch. Once cool, break it into pieces.

Melt the chocolate in a heatproof bowl set over a pan of simmering water, making sure the bottom of the bowl doesn't touch the water, then stir in most of the honeycomb pieces, reserving a few for decoration.

In a separate bowl, gently stir the cream into the mascarpone. Then stir two-thirds of the mix into the chocolate mix until just marbled. Spoon into small glasses or cups and top with the remaining cream mix and honeycomb pieces.

Cream and Soft Cheeses

Cream and Soft Cheeses

Once you have had a go at making some fresh cheeses, you should have a pretty good foundation of cheesemaking – when you have the curd right, you're on to a winner!

Soft and cream cheeses are the next step on your cheesemaking adventure; these are great cheeses to practise making, as firstly they are delicious (licking the bowl is my favourite part), but, more importantly, soft cheeses have a short ageing time, which means you can quickly find out if you love the cheese or would maybe like to tweak the recipe slightly. These cheeses can also be made in small batches, which is a good way to build your cheesemaking skills and get a feel for the craft without too much output. Cheeses that are unripened or unpressed fall under the category of soft cheese. Soft cheeses are described as 'runny', 'gooey' and 'wet'.

My advice would be to keep a record of how you are making the cheeses – make a note of what you have done at each step. This way, if you make a favourite cheese, you will be able to replicate it. This is an important process even for the most simple of cheeses, and if you get into the habit of doing it early on, it will soon become second nature and make life easier when you come to the trickier cheeses.

In this chapter there are also some delicious ways in which you can use your cream and soft cheeses. A soft cheese feels like a real treat and is wonderfully indulgent.

Brie de Meaux Dongé (left) is made by the Dongé family and is the best Brie money can buy. Full-flavoured, with a Camembert-like fruitiness, it's my go-to soft cheese that never lets me down.

Epoisses (front) is one of the world's smelliest cheeses – and also one of the most delicious. The cheese is so smelly that it is banned from being taken on all French public transport.

Neufchâtel is a stunning soft cheese, with a distinctive heart shape (right), said to have originated back when female cheesemakers moulded the cheese in this way to win the hearts of British soldiers.

Cream Cheese

This has got to be the most rewarding cheese in my eyes. I am a real bagel lover, and once I discovered how to make my own cream cheese, it changed my bagels forever. Forget about store-bought – fresh is best! This is a great recipe to experiment with; once you have made your first batch, don't be scared to play around – you could create a more sour cream cheese by adding more vinegar, or maybe add some herbs.

1 litre (1¾ pints/4 cups) double (heavy) cream

120ml (4 fl oz/½ cup) milk

2 tsp salt

60ml (2 fl oz/¼ cup) white wine vinegar

MAKES 150g (5oz)

You will need: a cheesecloth or muslin sheet and an instant-read thermometer

1 In a large pan, heat the cream, milk and salt over a medium heat, stirring gently to make sure it doesn't stick. Heat to 29°C (85°F), or until you start to see small bubbles.

2 Remove from the heat and let the mixture rest for a few minutes, then add the white wine vinegar and stir gently. Cover the mixture with a tea (dish) towel and leave to rest overnight at room temperature.

3 When you uncover your mixture, you should see the mix has begun to split. There should be a thick curd layer on top and a mildly watery layer of whey underneath.

4 Place the cheesecloth or muslin over a mixing bowl and pour the mixture in. Following the steps on pages 24–25, create a cloth bag and hang above a sink or the empty bowl.

5 Leave the mixture to drain for several hours, until you see that the whey has stopped dripping and the cheese feels firm. Remove it from its cloth and you have amazing ready-to-eat cream cheese. It will keep overnight in a sealed container in the refrigerator.

Salmon, Cream Cheese and Dill Pancakes

This is one of my favourite Saturday morning treats. I love making a fresh batch of pancake mix, leaving it to rest while I go and get ready for a busy day at the cheese shop, then popping down and making some delicious salmon and cream cheese pancakes. The best way to start the weekend in my eyes!

100g (3½oz) self-raising (self-rising) flour

230ml (8 fl oz/scant 1 cup) milk

1 egg

1 tbsp coconut oil

200g (7oz) cream cheese (see page 70)

4 tsp lemon juice

200g (7oz) smoked salmon

4 sprigs of fresh dill, chopped

1 lemon, thickly sliced

salt and freshly ground black pepper

SERVES 4

To make the basic batter mix, beat together the flour, milk and egg until smooth. Leave to stand for 1 hour; the longer the better when it comes to the batter.

Line a chopping 9cutting) board with greaseproof (wax) paper. Heat 1 teaspoon of coconut oil in a non-stick frying pan (skillet) over a medium heat. Add a ladleful of batter into the pan, swirling the pan so it covers the bottom in a thin layer. Cook the pancake for 30–60 seconds until lightly browned, then flip it over and cook on the other side. Remove from the pan and transfer to the paper.

Repeat with the remaining batter, heating more oil as necessary, until you have about 7 or 8 pancakes, layering with a sheet of paper between each pancake to prevent them sticking.

In a bowl, combine the cream cheese with the lemon juice and season with salt and pepper to taste, then spread over the pancakes. Top with generous slices of smoked salmon, a scattering of fresh dill and lemon slices, to serve.

Cottage Cheese

Cottage cheese is a super-easy, low-fat cheese. I love serving it with fruit for a delicious light breakfast or lunch. This dish is so ridiculously simple to make at home that there's no reason to pick up a tub at the supermarket. And you only need three main ingredients!

450ml (16 fl oz/scant 2 cups) milk

120ml (4 fl oz/½ cup) white wine vinegar

1 tsp salt

a little double (heavy) cream (optional)

MAKES 300g (10½oz)

You will need: a cheesecloth or muslin sheet and an instant-read thermometer

1 In a large saucepan, heat the milk to 87°C (190°F), stirring the milk frequently to make sure it doesn't stick to the bottom of the pan.

2 Once the milk reaches 87°C (190°F), turn off the heat and add the vinegar. Set aside to cool.

3 When cooled, line a colander with cheesecloth or muslin set over a bowl, then drain the mixture, separating the curds from the whey.

4 Transfer the drained curds to a bowl, sprinkle with the salt and stir well.

5 Now, this is all down to personal preference, but I love really creamy cottage cheese. So I like to add quite a lot of double (heavy) cream at this stage, but do taste as you go.

6 Mix to a smooth consistency, then serve immediately.

Brie

I love to make Brie. It is beautiful and challenging, and it is a truly rewarding cheese once you have mastered it. Now this may not happen right away, but give it time. And if you would like to challenge yourself further, why not try using goat's or ewe's milk?

3.8 litres (6¾ pints/16 cups) milk

¼ tsp mesophilic DVI MA culture

⅛ tsp Penicillium candidum

¼ tsp liquid rennet dissolved in 60ml (2 fl oz/¼ cup) cold water

salt for the brine

MAKES 2 x 150g (5oz) cheeses

You will need: an instant-read thermometer, a curd knife, 2 small round cheese moulds and a draining mat

1 Start by heating the milk in a large pan – slowly, slowly – to 29°C (85°F). Then add the culture, Penicillium candidum and rennet and mix well, making sure you stir right to the bottom of the pan. Remove from the heat and let it sit for 30 minutes.

2 After 30 minutes you should see that the curds and whey have separated. Cut the curd with a long knife into 1cm (½-inch) squares. Leave to rest for a further 10 minutes.

3 Place a tray or plate underneath the mat to catch the excess whey. Place the moulds on your mat, then carefully ladle the curds into the prepared moulds, to the top, being careful not to lose too much curd. Leave the curds to settle for about 20 minutes.

4 After 20 minutes, flip the mould over and let the curds sit for a further 30 minutes. Repeat this two more times, then leave the cheese to sit in the moulds on the mat overnight.

5 In the morning, remove the cheese from the mould and leave it on the mat to let the air get to it for 2–3 hours. It will shrink slightly. When the cheese is firm, wash it in brine, being sure to cover the whole cheese (see page 48). Leave to dry for 30–60 minutes.

6 To mature your cheese, place it in an area with a temperature of 10–14ºC (50–57ºF) so that the mould can develop. Keep an eye on the cheese; you should see the mould start to develop after 6–7 days and continue from there. After 13–14 days, the cheese should have a mild rind. Wrap it in greaseproof (wax) paper and leave for a further 10 days.

7 Now your cheese is ready to eat. But the longer you leave it, the stronger it will become, so experiment.

FROMAGERIE GANOT, FRANCE

Cheeses: Brie, Coulommiers

Fromagerie Ganot in Jouarre, east of Paris, is owned by world-famous affineur Stéphane Gay, best known for his AOC specialist cheeses such as the wonderful Brie de Meaux, Brie de Melun and Coulommiers. Throughout history, cheesemakers have sent their cheeses to affineurs like Stéphane, who matures the cheese for around 5 to 8 weeks in his temperature-controlled caves with perfect humidity. He also has a fantastic 'Brie Museum' on site, where you can learn all about the history of cheesemaking in the region – it is a wonderful place to visit!

Grilled Brie with Caramelized Apple and Honey

Forget boring cheese on toast. This recipe not only looks beautiful on the plate, but is also so delicious that you will be going back for seconds, thirds . . . The success of this recipe is down to good-quality ingredients: fresh bread, lovingly made Brie and a stunning honey of your choice. I love lavender or chestnut honey myself.

1 red crunchy apple
150g (5oz) Brie (see page 78)
50g (1¾oz) butter
2 slices of farmhouse bread
3 tbsp chestnut honey
pinch of salt and freshly ground black pepper

SERVES 2

Wash and core the apple and cut it into thin slices.

Cut the Brie in half, then cut each half into four slices.

In a pan, melt the butter and brown the apple slices for a few minutes until golden.

Lightly toast the slices of bread, then alternate the Brie and apple slices over the toast. Place under a preheated hot grill (broiler) for a couple of minutes to melt the cheese. Drizzle the honey over the cheese and apple slices, then season with salt and pepper.

STAR CHEESEMAKER
MEADOW CREEK DAIRY, USA

Cheeses: Grayson, Appalachian, Mountaineer

Nuzzled in the mountains of southwest Virginia, this family farm has been creating full-flavoured, ecologically friendly cheeses since 1980. These original raw milk cheeses are based on European cheesemaking techniques, carefully adapted by the farm. The Virginia mountains provide pure water, clean air and diverse, rich pastures, resulting in delicious cheeses such as the Grayson, a washed rind cheese. The texture is supple and fudgy, becoming silky as it warms; the rind is sweet, with nutty notes, originally inspired by a trip to Wales and Ireland in 2000.

Tartiflette

Can you handle potatoes and bacon cooked with a whole cheese? This classic French dish is not for the faint-hearted. It was created by reblochon cheesemakers as a way of selling more cheese, and in my shop it has certainly worked.

50g (1¾oz) butter, for greasing

1kg (2lb 3 oz) waxy potatoes, skin on

350g (12½oz) thick-cut bacon, cut into 1cm (½-inch) pieces

2 tbsp olive oil

2 large onions, thinly sliced

150ml (5 fl oz/scant ⅔ cup) white wine

450g (1lb) reblochon

150ml (5 fl oz/scant ⅔ cup) crème fraîche

salt and freshly ground black pepper

SERVES 6–8

Preheat the oven to 190°C (375°F/Gas Mark 5). Grease a large baking dish with the butter.

Boil the potatoes in salted water for 15–20 minutes until tender, drain then set aside to cool. In a large pan, fry the bacon in the oil over a medium-high heat until cooked. Add the onions with a little salt and pepper and cook until soft and golden. Add the white wine and cook off the alcohol until the liquid has reduced.

Cut the reblochon in half through the middle, then cut each half lengthways so you end up with four pieces. Set aside. Cut the potatoes into thick slices and lay half in the dish. Add the onion and bacon mix and finish with another layer of potatoes.

Spoon over the crème fraîche, then top with the reblochon. The four pieces should cover nearly all of the dish. Bake for 45 minutes until the cheese is bubbling.

Goat's Cheese

Goat's Cheese

Goat's cheese is the Marmite of cheeses. People love it or they hate it. For goat's cheese lovers, there are hundreds of varieties worldwide to try. And for those of you who haven't fallen in love yet, there is nothing quite like a homemade goat's cheese to change your mind.

Goat's cheese is one of the oldest cheeses in the world. I adore it for many reasons, one of them being that goat's cheese has about half the fat, cholesterol and calories of commercial cream cheese made from cow's milk, which it sometimes resembles in texture. This is due to the fact that the cheese curds produced by goat's milk are generally softer than those made from cow's milk, and the resulting cheese is more acidic.

The heavenly taste of goat's cheese has a lot to do with the way that goats, unlike cows, are 'browsers' rather than grazers, which means they eat a variety of grasses, weeds and wildflowers. The taste of the cheese often depends on the diet of the goat, so different areas – even within the same country – will produce different-tasting cheeses. They really are a product of their environment, which is why summer-season goat's cheese is so delicious; it's also a great season in which to have a go at making your own.

The production of goat's cheese follows many of the same basic steps as for other types of cheese. Once you have become confident with the basic goat's cheese recipe, don't be scared to experiment; each time I make a goat's cheese I do something different – mature it a little more, add new flavours or change the shape. Get creative!

Sainte Maure (left) is a classic goat's cheese from the Loire, with a very recognizable shape. It is so delicate and crumbly when young that it is held together by a thin straw. The fresh cheese is ashed, then ripened to produce a log that is both creamy, sharp and full-flavoured.

Crottin de Chavignol (centre) originates from Chavignol in the Loire. This small cylindrical goat's cheese has been produced since the sixteenth century and has a creamy, nutty taste. The more mature the cheese gets, the more it changes and develops, becoming harder with a more pronounced flavour.

Le Coup de Corne (right), from the Midi-Pyrénées, is traditionally made from cow's milk yet the clever cheesemakers of Fromagerie Beillevaire have also made a delicious goat's cheese version.

Creamy Goat's Cheese

Before making goat's cheese for the first time, I imagined milking a goat, then a dairy farm stocked with special equipment and ingredients . . . but making goat's cheese at home doesn't have to be complicated at all! This very simple version using citric acid and goat's milk is the perfect recipe to try, especially if you are just starting out. This recipe can also be made with lemon juice instead of citric acid.

1 tsp citric acid

2.25 litres (4 pints/9½ cups) goat's milk

2 tsp salt

MAKES 2 x 150g (5oz) cheeses

You will need: a cheesecloth or muslin sheet, an instant-read thermometer and two goat's cheese moulds (optional)

1 Dissolve the citric acid in 50ml (1¾ fl oz) cooled boiled water, stirring until completely dissolved.

2 Put the milk and citric acid mixture into a pan and stir well. Heat the milk over a medium heat to 85°C (185°F), stirring continuously.

3 Once the milk is at the required temperature, remove from the heat. You should be able to see that the curds and whey have separated, but don't worry if not. Set the pan aside, covered, for 30 minutes.

4 While the curds are resting, lay the cheesecloth or muslin over a colander in a bowl. When rested, gently pour in the curds. Drain, add the salt and mix gently.

5 Following the steps on pages 24–25, create a cloth bag and hang the curds over a sink or a bowl for about 1 hour to allow the whey to drain off.

6 Now you can shape the cheese by hand or ladle and press into moulds. This cheese can be eaten straight away or left in the refrigerator to firm up a little more. Store for up to 1 week in a sealed container in the refrigerator.

7 You can also add flavours to your
cheese – try using fresh herbs, chopped
sundried tomatoes or olives, or even
sweeter flavours like raspberries and
strawberries. You could also coat your
goat's cheese in herbs or black pepper.
Don't be afraid to experiment.

STAR CHEESEMAKER
KARDITSEL, BELGIUM

Cheeses: Florette, Mathilde, Cyriel, Corneel

In March 2015, cheesemakers Magda Bauweleers and Giedo De Snijder started at Karditsel. Sticking to the traditional craft of cheesemaking, they use organic goat's milk from the Goerenhof goat farm in Lummen, Belgium. Karditsel produces 13 varied and delicious cheeses, ranging from the Florette, a young goat's cheese with a thin layer of honey around the crust, topped with a mix of colourful, edible petals (it looks as good as it tastes); to the unusual Florence Maritime, a handmade goat's Brie coated with a thin layer of seaweed – the taste of salty seaweed on a bed of creaminess is superb; and the Corneel, a raw milk goat's cheese with rich flavours and a distinctive floral taste.

STAR CHEESEMAKER
CAPRIOLE, USA

Cheeses: Wabash Cannonball, Juliana, Sofia

Judy Schad has been making cheese since 1976, when she and her husband moved with their three young children from the city to a hill farm in southern Indiana. Judy makes over a dozen different goat's cheeses with smooth, creamy and rich flavours, some harder cheeses that are very light, lemony and slightly sharp. My favourite, the fantastically named Cannonball, is by far our most well-known, best-loved cheese, and for good reason. This expressive little sphere packs a punch! Beneath her wrinkly exterior lies a complexity not often found in such a young cheese.

Crumbly Goat's Cheese

This recipe makes a perfect batch of crumbly goat's cheese. By leaving the cheese to dry out for longer, it becomes drier and more crumbly than the smooth goat's cheese. You can form the cheese in a shaped mould (as below) or make a herbed roll. Here I have used ash, or activated charcoal powder (see page 222), which creates a beautiful and rich cheese.

1 tsp citric acid

2.25 litres (4 pints/9½ cups) goat's milk

1–2 tsp salt, to taste

ash, to finish

You will need: a cheesecloth or muslin sheet, an instant-read thermometer and two goat's cheese moulds (optional)

MAKES 2 x 150g (5oz) cheeses

1 Dissolve the citric acid in 50ml (1¾fl oz) cooled boiled water, stirring until completely dissolved.

2 Pour the goat's milk into a pan and heat slowly over a medium heat until the temperature reaches 87°C (190°F). Make sure you keep stirring the milk so that it doesn't stick to the bottom of the pan, and do not allow the milk to boil as this will affect the taste of the cheese.

3 You will see some steam and foam appear. Turn the heat down before the foam disappears and add the citric acid mixture. Stir and carry on cooking for a further minute over a low heat.

4 Remove from the heat and stir gently until you see the curds and whey separate. The curds will appear quite small and look different to cow's milk curds. Don't worry – keep at it.

5 Line a colander with a layer of cheesecloth or muslin. Slowly and gently pour the curds in. Leave to drain for 15 minutes.

6 Mix the salt into the curds and stir, then carefully gather the edges of the cloth together to create a bag shape. Press gently to get rid of any excess whey. Leave the cheese to sit for a further hour. The longer you leave the cheese, the firmer the end product will be. Then spoon into your moulds or shape by hand.

7 To finish, sprinkle the cheese with ash pushed through a tea strainer. Store in a sealed container in the refrigerator for up to 1 week.

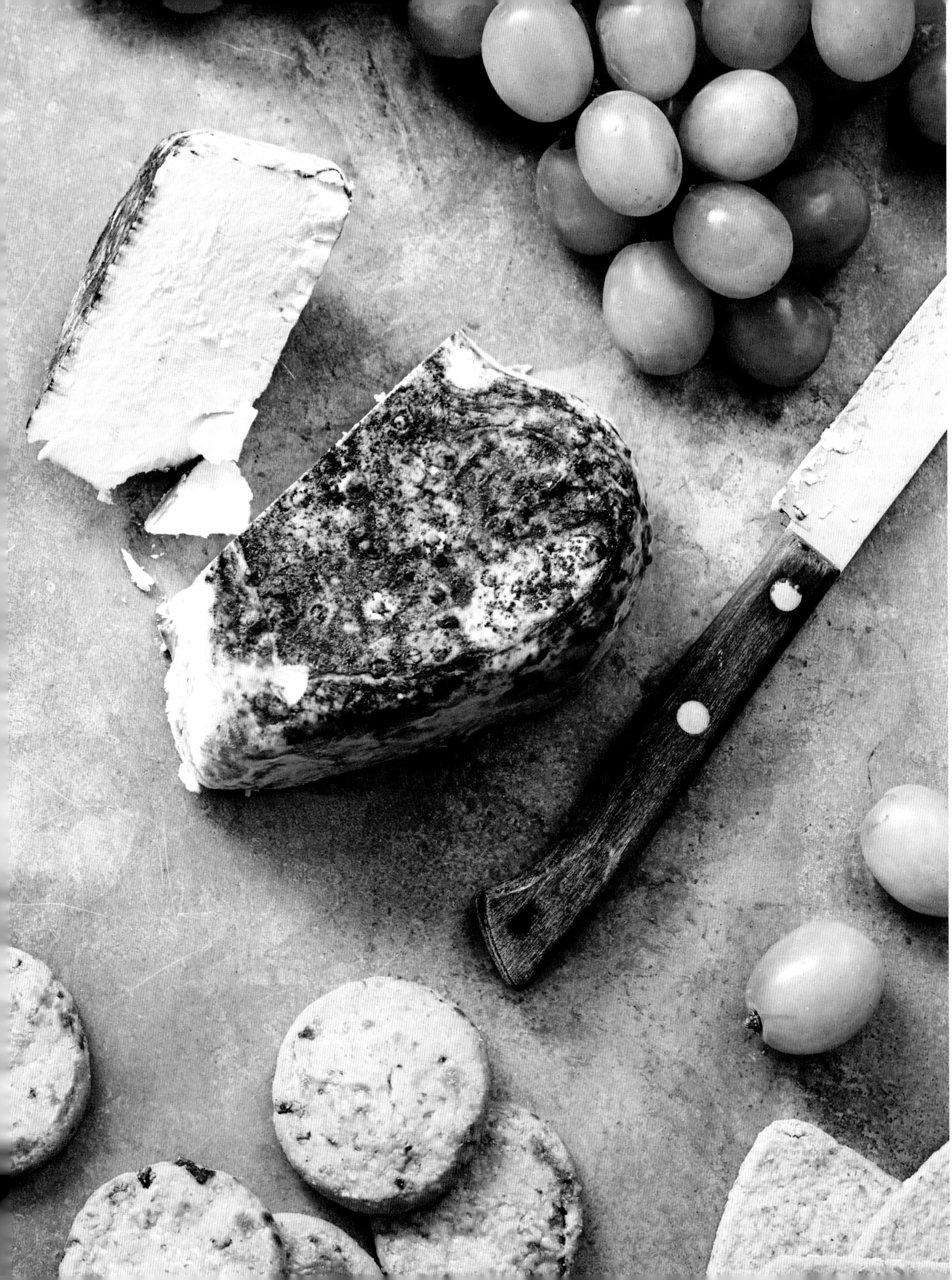

Courgette (Zucchini) and Goat's Cheese Tart

Nestled in the heart of this flaky puff pastry tart is a mouthwatering combination of salty goat's cheese, succulent courgettes (zucchini) and creamy crème fraîche. Perfect to serve at a summer party, as it is great for sharing.

2 tbsp olive oil

2 courgettes (zucchini), cut into 1cm (½-inch) slices

200ml (7 fl oz/generous ¾ cup) crème fraîche

2 eggs

250g (9oz) crumbly goat's cheese (see page 92)

1 sheet of puff pastry

salt and freshly ground black pepper

SERVES 6

Preheat the oven to 200°C (400°F/Gas Mark 6).

Heat the olive oil in a pan, then add the courgette (zucchini) slices and cook for about 10 minutes until browned.

In a mixing bowl, combine the crème fraîche and the eggs, then crumble in the goat's cheese and add a little salt and pepper.

Lay the pastry dough over a 30 x 20cm (12 x 8-inch) baking tray (sheet), then use a fork to make small holes in the pastry dough. Place half the courgette (zucchini) slices over the pastry dough, then pour over the egg and cheese mixture, and finish with the rest of the courgette (zucchini) slices on top of the tart.

Bake for 30–40 minutes until browned. The tart can be eaten warm or left to cool. Serve with a rocket (arugula) and red onion salad.

STAR CHEESEMAKER
CYPRESS GROVE, USA

Cheeses: Humboldt Fog, Bermuda Triangle

Cheesemaker Mary Keehn became interested in Alpine dairy goats while searching for a healthy source of milk for her young children. In 1983, Mary officially launched Cypress Grove. She tasted and tested and learned from the masters and makers of Brie, Camembert, Morbier and more in France, and suffice to say, Mary found her muse. At the time, commercial goat's cheese production was nearly unheard of in the US, but Mary and a few other goat's cheesemakers began to spread the word. Today, Cypress Grove is known worldwide for its fresh, soft and aged cheeses.

Goat's Cheese and Spinach Filo Swirls

This is my take on the Greek spanakopita, a crispy filo (phyllo) pastry with a wonderfully cheesy spinach filling. The traditional spanakopita spiral is made with feta, but I love the tanginess that goat's cheese brings to it.

cooking oil spray

2 large onions, thinly sliced

1 tsp light brown sugar

300g (10½oz) fresh spinach, cooked and drained

4 small sheets of filo (phyllo) pastry

50g (1¾oz) creamy or crumbly goat's cheese (see page 88 or 92)

½ tsp freshly ground black pepper

handful of black sesame seeds

SERVES 4

Preheat the oven to 190°C (375°F/Gas Mark 5).

Spray a little oil into a non-stick frying pan (skillet) over a low heat and cook the onions for 5 minutes, then add the sugar and cook for a further 5–6 minutes until the onions are golden brown. Stir through the spinach, then set aside to cool.

Lay out your pastry sheets and divide the onion and spinach mixture equally between them. Spread out evenly over the sheets, then top with the cheese. Season with the black pepper. Roll into sausage shapes and then into coils.

Spray a baking tray with oil and lay the coils on the tray (sheet). Bake for 8–10 minutes until golden brown.

Top with the sesame seeds, and serve.

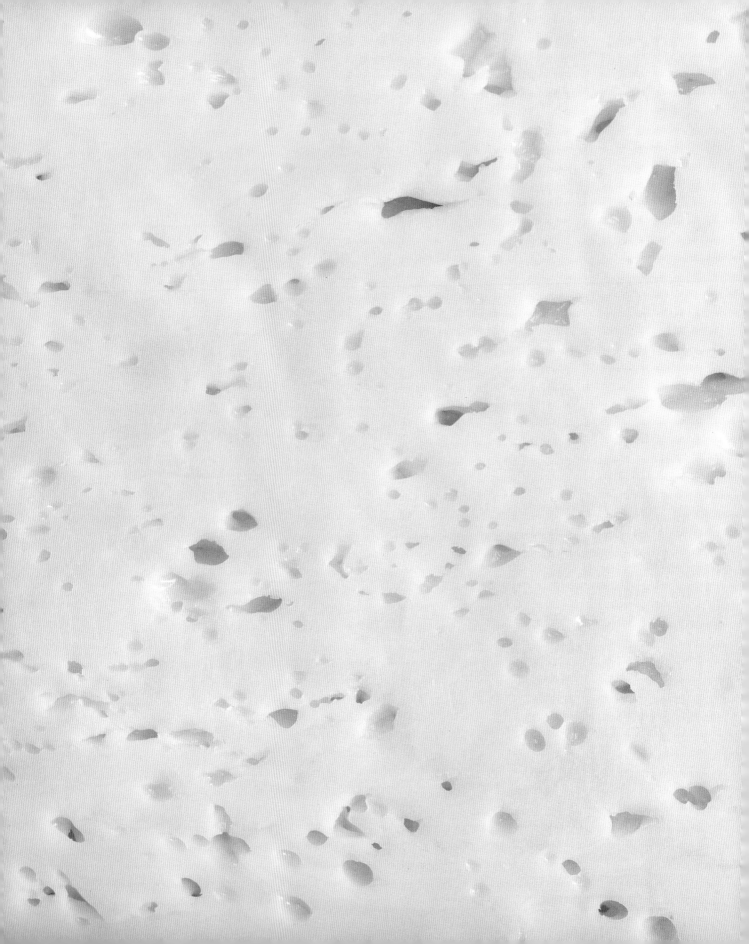

Semi-hard Cheese

Semi-hard Cheese

In this chapter we are moving on to semi-hard cheese, which will challenge the cheesemaking skills you have picked up so far. Here you will learn the art of 'affinage' – ageing your cheese – which is very important when making this style of cheese.

'Affinage' simply means 'to refine', whether it is washing, piercing and turning the cheese, making sure it is not too dry, and not too wet, that it has enough air, but not too much air. It really is an art, and it all depends on the style of the cheese. It is a great skill to learn and build on.

What happens to the cheese in this maturing stage is loss of moisture, the breaking down of proteins and fats, and the development of rind, texture and flavour. Your cheese is like a living thing and should be treated as such: think of it as a smelly pet that needs care and attention.

When making cheese at home, I sometimes use the water bath method – for the Swiss Cheese on page 112, for example. This is where a stainless steel pan of milk is placed in a warm water bath so that the water around the pan ensures that any temperature changes are gradual. This is another good skill to pick up and gives you a greater level of control.

It is important to keep a record of ageing techniques, temperatures and the environment in which you make your cheese; all these elements will make a difference to the final product.

Once you have mastered these skills, you will be able to mature your own cheeses and, over time can adjust the recipes to reflect any changes you may have made; this way you will create your own customized cheeses.

Raclette (left), is the best melting cheese, with a real buttery flavour. Its production dates back over 100 years. Look out for the recipe on page 118, which shows how to use this cheese in the most delicious way possible.

Morbier (right), a moreish creamy French cheese, is immediately identified due to the black layer of tasteless ash, which cuts horizontally through the centre of the cheese. This was traditionally used to keep the milk fresh: the cheese was made up of the morning and evening milk, and due to a lack of refrigeration, the ash kept the morning milk fresh.

Hereford Hop (front) is made by the world-famous cheesemaker Charles Martell, the maker of Stinking Bishop. This is his full-fat creamy cow's cheese, encrusted with toasted beer hops, which give a delicious edge to the flavour.

Paneer

Paneer is the most fantastically easy cheese to make, using ingredients you will have in your kitchen. It is a deliciously fresh-tasting cheese, and the great thing about it is that there is no ageing or culturing. Paneer is a very important ingredient in Indian cooking, and is used in many vegetarian dishes; it has a wonderful milky flavour, with a crumbly texture ideal for frying, grilling (broiling) or barbecuing. You can buy paneer at most supermarkets, but homemade fresh paneer tastes much better and is far superior to the mass-produced cheese you can buy off the shelf.

2.3 litres (4 pints/9¾ cups) milk

2 tbsp lemon juice

½ tsp salt

MAKES 250g (9oz)

You will need: a cheesecloth or muslin sheet, an instant-read thermometer and 2–3 tin cans or a cheese press

1 Put the milk into a saucepan over a medium heat and simmer until the temperature reaches 93°C (200°F). Be sure to stir occasionally to make sure the milk doesn't burn or stick to the bottom of the pan. When ready, the milk should look foamy.

2 Remove the milk from the heat and stir in the lemon juice. It should start to curdle.

3 Leave the milk to stand for 10 minutes, then cover with the pan lid and let it stand for a further 10 minutes. The curds should have completely separated and the remaining water should be yellow in colour.

4 Place a sieve (fine-mesh strainer) over a mixing bowl and line it with the cheesecloth or muslin. Carefully scoop the cheese curds into the sieve (fine-mesh strainer), letting all the whey collect in the mixing bowl below.

5 To remove any excess whey, gather the cloth in your hands and squeeze out all the remaining liquid. Open the cloth out again, sprinkle the salt over the curds and stir through.

6 Keeping the curds in the cloth, move them into a baking dish and shape them into a rough triangle. Wrap the cloth tightly around and over the top of the cheese and place a large plate on top. Weigh down the plate with two or three tin cans, or use a cheese press, and leave for 1 hour. Once pressed, the paneer is ready to eat, or it will keep wrapped in the refrigerator for up to 2 weeks.

Paneer-Stuffed Peppers

These colourful stuffed peppers make for a satisfying vegetarian dinner. The homemade paneer's mild, milky flavour and dense crumbly texture go beautifully with the strong, spicy flavours in this dish.

4 large red or green (bell) peppers

4 tbsp coconut oil

2 tsp cumin seeds

1 red onion, chopped

2 handfuls of frozen peas

100g (3½oz) green beans, chopped

½ tsp ground ginger

3 large tomatoes, finely chopped

½ tsp turmeric powder

½ red chilli, chopped

2 tsp ground coriander

250g (9oz) paneer (see page 102), cubed

5 tbsp double (heavy) cream

handful of fresh coriander (cilantro), chopped

salt and freshly ground black pepper

SERVES 4

Preheat the oven to 190°C (375°F/Gas Mark 5).

Slice the tops off the peppers, deseed them, then replace the tops. Place the peppers on a baking sheet, spoon over 1 tbsp of the coconut oil and bake for about 25 minutes, or until softened. Remove from the oven and set aside to cool.

Meanwhile, heat the remaining coconut oil in a non-stick saucepan. Add the cumin seeds and fry for 30 seconds until you can smell the cumin.

Add the chopped onion and cook for a few minutes until golden brown, then add your peas, beans, ginger, tomatoes, a pinch of the salt and the spices and simmer for 10 minutes, or until the tomatoes have completely softened.

Add the paneer, then 100ml (3½ fl oz/scant ½ cup) water and stir until mixed. Add the cream and a pinch of black pepper. Simmer until the mixture has heated all the way through. Add the fresh coriander (cilantro) and continue to simmer for a further 5 minutes, adding tablespoons of water as necessary to stop the sauce sticking as the paneer will absorb quite a lot of the liquid.

Preheat the grill (broiler). While it is heating up, fill the baked peppers with the mixture. Grill (broil) the peppers for a couple of minutes until they bubble then replace the tops. Serve with tzatziki or a salad of your choice.

Paneer Summer Rolls with Peanut Butter Dipping Sauce

You can't go wrong with these rolls. They are the perfect light, healthy meal or snack, with the freshness of a salad. Wrapped in rice paper and filled with fresh ingredients, summer rolls can also be hearty. Vietnamese in origin, they are typically stuffed with shrimp, pork or chicken, but I love using paneer. I also add edible flowers to mine, for no other reason than they look so beautiful! These are perfect nibbles to serve at a party and to impress your guests.

Paneer spring rolls

100g (3½oz) paneer (see page 102)

10 rice paper summer roll wrappers

handful of edible flowers

1 large carrot, peeled and cut into thin strips

2 red (bell) peppers, deseeded and cut into thin strips

5 spring onions (scallions), cut into thin strips

1 avocado, stoned, peeled and sliced

handful of fresh coriander (cilantro) leaves, chopped

Peanut butter dipping sauce

1 tbsp sesame oil

1 tbsp garlic-infused oil

1 tbsp soy sauce

2 tbsp sweet chilli sauce

3 tbsp smooth peanut butter

2 tbsp lime juice

SERVES 2–3

Mix together all the sauce ingredients in a bowl and set aside.

Chop the paneer into small pieces and fry in a non-stick frying pan (skillet) over a medium heat for about 5 minutes, until crispy. Set aside to cool.

To make the rolls, simply place the rice paper wrappers into a bowl of warm water for 10 seconds. Once soft, lay some edible flowers face down in the centre of each wrapper so that they show through the rice paper. Top with a mixture of the vegetable strips, avocado, paneer and coriander (cilantro), and drizzle a teaspoon of the peanut sauce over each one.

Fold the top and the bottom of the wrappers over the filling, then roll up from the right side.

Serve the rolls with the leftover sauce for dipping.

Paneer, Potato and Coconut Curry

This has got to be my favourite recipe in the book, mainly for sentimental reasons, as every time I cook this flavour-packed curry I think of my amazing dad. He taught me this recipe when I first took an interest in cooking, and it is the best dish he makes. This will always remind me of our big family meals, with a pot of this gorgeous curry in the middle of the table, lots of naan bread, rice and homemade raita. I hope you love it as much as I do.

4 tbsp coconut oil

3 dried red chillies, chopped

1 tsp mustard seeds

10–12 curry leaves

2 onions, finely chopped

4 tomatoes, finely chopped

2 tsp ground coriander

1 tsp turmeric powder

1 tsp garam masala

250g (9oz) paneer (see page 102), cubed

7–8 potatoes, peeled and cut into bite-sized chunks

400ml (14 fl oz/1⅔ cups) coconut milk

3 tbsp desiccated (dried shredded) coconut

1 tsp red chilli powder

100g (3½oz) frozen peas

handful of fresh coriander (cilantro) leaves

salt

SERVES 4-6

Heat 2 tablespoons of the coconut oil in a large saucepan. When the oil is nice and hot, add the chillies, mustard seeds and curry leaves and cook for a few minutes.

Add the chopped onions and cook for 8–10 minutes until the onions are golden brown. Add the chopped tomatoes, mix well and cook for about 4 minutes. Add the ground coriander, turmeric, garam masala and a little salt to the pan. Mix well and cook for about 5 minutes until the tomatoes and spices are cooked through.

While this is cooking, heat the remaining coconut oil in a frying pan (skillet) and cook the paneer for 3–4 minutes until golden brown.

Add the potatoes to the pan of tomatoes and stir to coat in the onion and tomato mixture. Pour in the coconut milk, coconut and chilli powder, along with about 120ml (4 fl oz/½ cup) water. Bring to the boil then reduce the heat and simmer, covered, for 25–30 minutes, stirring occasionally, until the potatoes are just tender. Add the peas and the cheese and mix through. Sprinkle with the coriander (cilantro) leaves.

Serve with rice and naan bread, with mango chutney and yoghurt on the side.

Swiss Cheese

This is a recipe that will put your cheesemaking skills to the test. You may not master it on the first go, but keep trying because the end result is well worth it. The Swiss have a long history of making cheese, dating back 2,000 years, and now you can recreate a little piece of that in the comfort of your own home. Again, make notes as you make the cheese, so you have a record of the best version you produce.

7.5 litres (13 pints/32 cups) milk

⅛ tsp MM100 mesophilic culture or Thermo B culture (for a buttery flavour)

1 tsp + 1 tbsp calcium chloride

pinch of Propionic shermanii (the stuff that creates the holes)

1.5ml liquid rennet

1kg (2¼lb) salt

1 tsp white wine vinegar

MAKES 500g (1lb 1¾oz)

You will need: a cheesecloth or muslin sheet, an instant-read thermometer, a curd knife and a large cheese mould

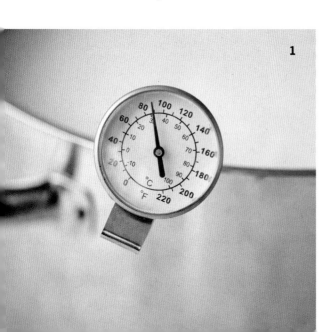

1

1   In a large saucepan, heat the milk to 30°C (86°F). I do this not over direct heat but by setting the pan in a warm water bath in the sink. Stir the milk gently so it warms through evenly. Once the milk has reached temperature, add the required culture and ½tsp calcium chloride and leave for a minute or two.

2   Now add the propionic acid and let this sit for a further 2 minutes, then stir thoroughly. Leave the milk to sit in the warm water bath for 45 minutes, making sure you maintain the 30°C (86°F) temperature throughout. Add hot water to the sink if necessary.

3   Next, add the rennet to the milk, cover and leave to sit for another 45 minutes. You will see the milk thicken and the rennet work its magic.

4   Once the 45 minutes are up, you will see the curds have formed. Now it's time to cut your curds, first into 2.5cm (1-inch) pieces, then 1cm (½-inch) pieces, then 5mm (¼-inch) pieces, then finally into 3mm (⅛-inch) pieces. Try and do this as evenly as possible. Let the curds rest for 5 minutes.

5   Next, carefully pour off the whey.

6   Now it's time to cook the curds, which will dry them out. You will need to slowly increase the heat to 49°C (120°F); you can do this by slowly adding hot water directly into the curds. This should take about 15–20 minutes. The final amount of water added should be roughly equal to the whey that was taken out. Stir the

7

curds for 30–45 minutes to create the perfect dryness. The curds should be cooked well, so if you broke into them, they would be firm throughout and bouncy to touch.

7 Once this is done, leave the curds to settle for 20 minutes. Set a sieve (fine-mesh strainer) over a bowl, line it with cheesecloth or muslin and set aside. Carefully drain out enough water from the pan so that the cheese curds are just covered. With your hands, press the curds gently to one side of the pan, so they are together. Once you see the curds form a mass, remove the remaining liquid and transfer the curds into your cloth-lined strainer.

8 Gather the cloth at the top to form a bag, then press the curds into a solid mass, squeezing out the whey. Transfer these curds into your cheese mould.

9 Once the cheese is in the mould it's time to press it, with a weight of about 2.5kg (5½lb) set on top of a plate on top of the cheese. Every hour or so, turn the cheese and add the weight again, each time adding a little more weight. After 5 hours you should end up with about 5.5kg (12lb) of weight on the cheese. Keep the cheese somewhere warm while doing this.

10 Now it is time to move the cheese to a cooler environment, about 11°C (52°F). Remove the weights and leave to rest for 12 hours.

11 Once you have left your cheese overnight, you can start preparing your salt bath for washing it. You will need a large bowl or bucket. Lay the cheese in the bottom and add 1kg (2¼lbs) of salt, 1 tablespoon of calcium chloride and 1 teaspoon of white wine vinegar. Top up with 4.5 litres (8 pints/19 cups) of water. Leave the cheese in the salt bath for 3 hours, turning it halfway through and adding a little more salt to the surface.

12 Pour out the brine and rinse the cheese with clean water. Leave the cheese to dry off, uncovered, at a temperature of 10–13°C (50–55°F) for 3 weeks. Every few days, turn the cheese over and wash with a damp cloth to stop mould.

13 Now it's time to age your cheese. It should be kept in an area that is about 18–21°C (65–70°F) for 2–3 weeks; in this time the holes will develop. Try to turn the cheese every few days, as this will stop the moisture forming on one side only. After this time, move the cheese to a cool room at 7–10°C (45–50°F) and let it mature for 1 month. Once cut it will keep for up to 1 month in the refrigerator. Left intact it will continue to mature and the flavour will strengthen.

12

STAR CHEESEMAKER
BELLELAY, SWITZERLAND

Cheese: Tête de Moine

Tête de Moine, meaning 'monks head', was said to be created as early as 1192 by the monks of the monastery at Bellelay. The recipe was later passed on to local farmers and cheesemakers, whose descendants still produce the cheese today. Production has spread to many small dairies throughout the area of the Bernese Jura. What I love most about Tête de Moine is that you can use a special cutter called a girolle. This shaves the cheese into 'cheese flowers' and helps to release the aroma and flavours.

Cheese Straws

These delicious cheesy straws are a great way to use up odd bits and bobs of cheese in the refrigerator. They're perfect for dipping, but just as good on their own.

1 sheet of puff pastry

flour, for dusting

1 egg

1 tsp milk

total of 100g (3½oz) Swiss cheese (see page 112), Emmental and Gruyère, grated and combined

salt and freshly ground black pepper

MAKES ABOUT 24

Preheat the oven to 180°C (350°F/Gas Mark 4) and line a baking sheet with non-stick baking (parchment) paper.

Lay out the puff pastry on a lightly floured surface. Combine the egg and milk in a small bowl, then brush the egg wash over the pastry dough. Scatter the grated cheese mix all over and add a pinch of salt and pepper.

Using a sharp knife, cut the dough into two pieces horizontally. Then cut each piece into 1cm (½-inch) wide strips to make about 24 straws. You can leave them as straight straws or take both ends and twist to create a cheese twist.

Transfer the straws to the prepared baking sheet and cook for about 5 minutes, until golden brown, then place on a wire (cooling) rack to cool.

STAR CHEESEMAKER
JOSEPH PACCARD, FRANCE

Cheeses: Tomme, Reblochon

The Paccard family have been refining and maturing cheeses for dairy farmers for the last 27 years in their caves in Manigod, France, in completely natural surroundings using traditional methods. Each year, 240 tonnes (metric tons) of reblochon pass through the caves here. Paccard refines and matures several other important cheeses with AOP status from this region, including Tomme de Savoie Fermier, Tome des Bauges Beaufort and Chevrotin, a goat's cheese reblochon. There are also tours of the caves and a shop on site where one can buy and taste cheeses.

Easy Raclette at Home

Raclette is an all-time favourite of mine, bringing back wonderful memories of being in Val d'Isère at ski school and coming in from the snow to this melty potato heaven. Raclette is a particularly popular dish in the Swiss Alps and other ski regions, which is where this wonderful cheese comes from.

2 tbsp olive oil

1 onion, thinly sliced

100g (3½oz) waxy potatoes, such as new potatoes

8 cornichons

6 pearl onions

150g (5oz) raclette cheese, sliced

salt

SERVES 2

Heat the oil in a pan over a medium heat and add the sliced onions. Gently cook the onion for about 7–8 minutes until golden brown, then set aside.

Meanwhile, cook the potatoes in a pan of salted boiling water for 10–12 minutes until cooked but not soft. Drain and leave to sit in a colander for a few minutes to get rid of any excess water, then cut into bite-sized pieces. Combine the potatoes with the onions in the pan, then transfer to two small heatproof dishes. Divide the cornichons and pearl onions between the two.

Preheat the grill (broiler) to a medium heat. Lay the sliced raclette over the potato and onions, then cook for about 2 minutes until the cheese bubbles – keep a close eye on it. Serve and eat straight away.

Halloumi

This super-easy halloumi is so delicious, but a far cry from the salty, squeaky halloumi cheese we're used to. It takes less than two hours to prepare (and the end result is a fantastic homemade Greek cheese!

8 litres (14 pints/34 cups) milk

½ tsp liquid rennet, diluted in 60ml (2 fl oz/¼ cup) cold water

½ tsp calcium chloride, diluted in 60ml (2 fl oz/¼ cup) cold water

rock salt or cheese salt

MAKES 300g (10½oz)

You will need: a cheesecloth or muslin sheet, an instant-read thermometer and a curd knife

1 Pour the milk into a large saucepan and heat to 32°C (90°F), stirring continuously. Once it reaches the required temperature, add the rennet and calcium chloride and remove from the heat. Stir well and cover with the pan lid for 30–40 minutes to allow the curds to set.

2 Cut the curds into 1.25cm (½-inch) cubes using a curd knife, then leave to rest for a further 5 minutes.

3 Return to a low heat and slowly heat to 38°C (100°F). This should take about 15–20 minutes. Set the curds aside to rest for 10 minutes until they start to become solid.

4 Place the cheesecloth or muslin in a sieve (fine-mesh strainer) set over a bowl, spoon in the curds and drain for about 5 minutes until there is no whey left, squeezing the cloth to remove any remaining whey. Retain the whey in the bowl below and set aside.

5 Carefully transfer the curds in the cloth onto a large chopping board and fold the cloth into a roughly flat shape (it doesn't have to be perfect). Make sure the cloth is completely covering the cheese so the curds won't spill out. Place a second board or a plate on top and add some weight (I usually add about 5kg/11lb). You can use a cheese press if you have one. Leave for 10 minutes, then flip the cheese over and return the weight for another 20 minutes.

6 While the curds are being pressed, return the whey to the hob (stovetop) and heat to 90°C (194°F). Discard any remaining curd that floats to the top.

7

8

7 Remove the weight and open up the cloth carefully. Cut the curds into 10 x 15cm (4- x 6-inch) pieces, then place them into the hot whey set over a low heat. They should sink to the bottom, but after 45 minutes of gentle cooking they will float to the top. Remove from the heat and set aside for another 15 minutes.

8 Remove the cheese and place it in a shallow dish filled with rock or cheese salt. Coat with the salt, and while the cheese is still hot, fold it in half and leave it to drain in a colander for 1 hour.

9 Place in an airtight container in the refrigerator and leave 24 hours before using so that the salt permeates the cheese. Consume within 1 week. Another method of storage is to vacuum pack the cheese and keep it for up to 6 months in the refrigerator – not that it will last that long as it is too yummy.

Warm Puy Lentil, Cherry Tomato and Halloumi Salad

The lentils, salty halloumi cheese and rich, juicy tomatoes all work together in this salad to create a light but flavoursome dish that takes seconds to make. I make this in the cheese shop for a quick, tasty lunch.

250g (9oz) cherry tomatoes, halved

½ red onion, finely sliced

½ garlic clove, crushed

juice of ½ lemon

1 tbsp extra-virgin olive oil

150g (5oz) Puy lentils, rinsed

150g (5oz) halloumi (see page 120), cut into thick slices

small bunch of fresh coriander (cilantro), roughly chopped

salt and freshly ground black pepper

SERVES 2

Toss the tomatoes, red onion, garlic, lemon juice and olive oil in a large serving bowl.

Cook the Puy lentils in a pan of salted water for 20–25 minutes until just tender, then drain and add to the bowl. Season well and toss all the ingredients together.

Preheat the grill (broiler), then grill (broil) the halloumi slices for a few minutes until golden. Stir the coriander (cilantro) through the lentils and serve with the halloumi.

Feta

I adore a fresh feta cheese salad, so I love being able to whip up a batch of feta quickly and easily at home. Once you have mastered it, it's a really great cheese to experiment with – you can add different kinds of herbs, vegetables or even olives. Have fun with it.

120ml (4 fl oz/½ cup) live natural (plain) low-fat yoghurt

3.8 litres (6¾ pints/16 cups) milk

¼ tsp lipase powder

¾ tsp calcium chloride

¼ tsp liquid rennet

50g (1¾oz) salt

fresh herbs, for sprinkling (optional)

MAKES 400g (14oz)

You will need: a cheesecloth or muslin sheet, an instant-read thermometer, a curd knife, a draining mat and a square feta mould

1 In a small bowl, mix the yoghurt with 120ml (4 fl oz/½ cup) of the milk.

2 Put the rest of the milk in a large pan over a low heat and heat slowly, the slower the better. You are looking for the milk to reach 32°C (90°F). Stir the milk from time to time so it doesn't stick to the bottom of the pan. This should take 15–20 minutes. Remove from the heat, stir in the yoghurt mixture, cover and leave for 1 hour.

3 While this is resting, mix the lipase powder with 60ml (2 fl oz/¼ cup) water and leave this to sit for 30 minutes, then stir in the calcium chloride and liquid rennet and mix to a smooth paste.

4 Set the pan of milk back over a low heat, then add the lipase, calcium choride and rennet mix. Stir in well. Heat the milk to 35°C (95°F), then turn off the heat and cover the pan. Leave it to sit for 2–3 hours to allow time for the curds to set.

5 Once set, cut the curds into 1cm (½-inch) squares with your curd knife, right down to the bottom of the pan. Set the pan back over a low heat and heat the curds for 5 minutes. Stir the curds until the temperature reaches 35°C (95°F), then turn off the heat and cover the pot once again, leaving the curds to sit for 1 hour. Stir occasionally.

5

8

6 Set a sieve (fine-mesh strainer) over a bowl, line it with cheesecloth or muslin and pour in the curds. Allow the whey to drain off, then set aside 500ml (2 cups) of drained whey. Store in the refrigerator for later.

7 Set another strainer over a large bowl and line it with two layers of cheesecloth or muslin. Pour in the curds and drain off the whey for a further 30 minutes. Following the steps on pages 24–25, create a cloth bag and hang the curds over a sink or bowl for about 2–3 hours.

8 The curds should now be more firm and solid. Scoop the curds into a square feta mould (open at top and bottom) set over a draining mat on a plate, packing it well.

9 At this point, sprinkle a few pinches of salt over the top and bottom of the cheese, along with some fresh herbs, if desired. Flip the mould over to do this.

10 Cover and leave to sit at room temperature for 3 days. Turn the feta in the mould daily and add more salt. Each day, pour off any whey as it collects in the plate. Remove from the mould.

9

10

11 To wash the cheese, mix 50g (1¾oz) salt with the reserved whey in a bowl until completely dissolved. Submerge the cheese in the mixture, making sure you cover it completely. Refrigerate the cheese for at least 1 week before eating, but you can leave it for up to 5 weeks. The longer you leave it, the more mature and stronger-tasting the cheese will be.

Courgette (Zucchini) and Feta Fritters with Yoghurt Dip

These little beauties make a lovely snack – the perfect recipe for your homemade feta. I first made these fritters because I wanted to use up some leftover veggies from the refrigerator. You could also use carrots, potatoes, and even sweetcorn instead of courgettes (zucchini).

2 medium courgettes (zucchini)

1 tbsp salt

1 garlic clove, crushed

1 tbsp coconut oil

½ tsp freshly ground black pepper

2 tbsp chopped fresh dill

2 eggs

1 tsp baking powder

180g (6¼oz) panko breadcrumbs

250g (9oz) feta (see page 126), crumbled

Yoghurt dip

240g (8½oz) Greek yoghurt

2 tbsp lemon juice

1–2 tsp chopped fresh dill

SERVES 2

Peel and grate the courgettes (zucchini) into a sieve (fine-mesh strainer) or set over a bowl. Sprinkle with the salt and stir, then leave to sit for 20 minutes. This will get rid of some of the moisture.

After 20 minutes, use your hands to squeeze out as much liquid from the grated courgette (zucchini) as you can, until it feels dry.

Preheat the oven to 180°C (350°F/Gas Mark 4), and line a baking sheet with non-stick baking (parchment) paper.

In a bowl, combine the drained courgettes (zucchini) with the garlic, coconut oil, pepper, dill, eggs, baking powder, breadcrumbs and feta.

Take about 2 tablespoons of the mixture and shape it into a patty, then place it on the prepared baking sheet. Repeat with the rest of the mixture, leaving some space between each patty.

Bake for 20–30 minutes, until golden.

While the fritters are cooking, make the dip. Combine the yoghurt, lemon juice, dill and salt, to taste, in a bowl. Serve alongside the cooked fritters with some rocket (arugula) salad.

STAR CHEESEMAKER
KOSTARELOS DAIRY, GREECE

Cheeses: 6- and 12-month barrel-aged Feta

Renowned for their feta and goat's cheese, the Kostarelos family have been cheesemaking since 1937, the business having now been passed down to Kyriakos and Nikos, the third generation, who have stepped up to continue the legacy. They have found a wonderful balance between traditional and modern cheesemaking techniques. They say the secret to their success is largely tied to observing old Greek farming techniques, using small herds that roam freely around the meadows of Karistos, south of Evia, to achieve the similar tastes and characteristics that their ancestors did.

Beetroot (Beet), Mint, Fennel and Feta Salad

Beetroot (beets) and fennel are two of my favourite ingredients. This salad is lovely, and a refreshingly crisp and crunchy addition to any meal.

2 tbsp honey

3 tbsp lemon juice

9 tbsp extra-virgin olive oil

2 heads of fennel

2 handfuls of fresh mint leaves

3 lemons

300g (10½oz) feta (see page 126), crumbled

800g (1lb 12oz) cooked beetroot (beets), sliced

salt and freshly ground black pepper

SERVES 2

In a small bowl, whisk together the honey, lemon juice and olive oil. Season with salt and pepper and set aside.

Trim the base and top of each fennel head and halve them. Slice as finely as you can into shreds and place in a large mixing bowl with the mint.

Peel the lemons, then halve lengthways and finely slice into half-moons. Discard any seeds and add the lemon slices to the fennel. Toss in half the lemon and honey dressing, then crumble in the feta.

Place the beetroot (beets) in a separate bowl. Toss in the remainder of the dressing and season to taste. Gently mix the two salads together and serve.

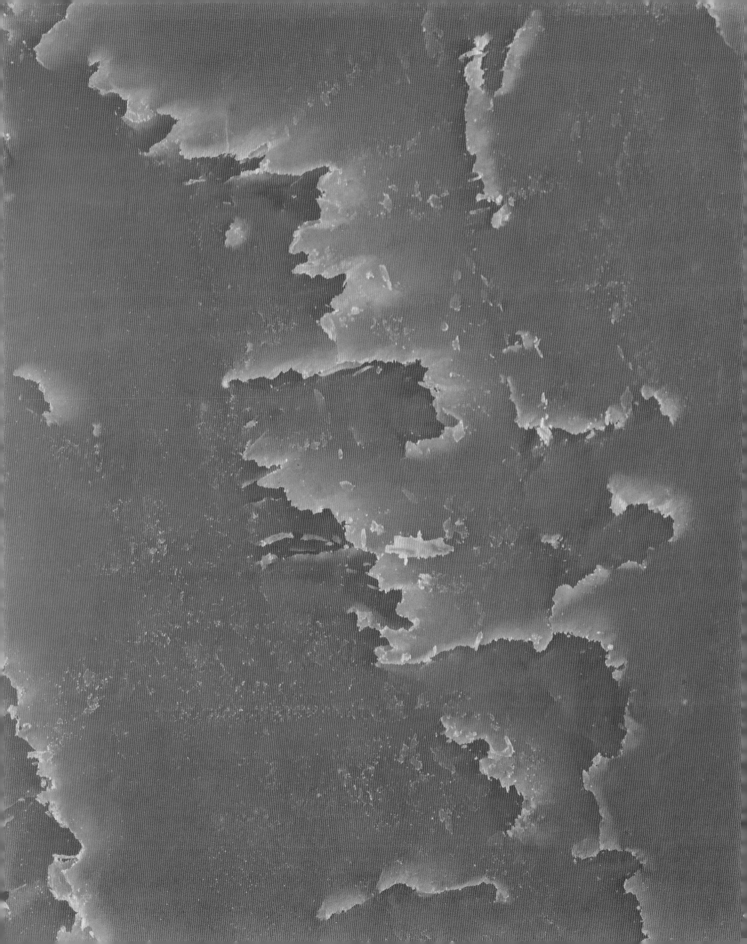

Hard Cheese

Hard Cheese

Now for something a little bit harder . . . in both texture and technique.
I absolutely adore hard cheese. My favourite childhood snack was a good
Cheddar and fresh apples. Some of the best cheeses in the world fall into
this category, such as stunning aged Comté from the Jura mountains in
France, or beautiful rich, strong Cheddar from the rolling hills of Somerset.

My recipes for hard cheese have been inspired by some of the
world's best cheesemakers. After visiting their farms and dairies,
I have picked up wonderful tricks of the trade that inspired me
to start making hard cheese at home. Hard cheese is a labour
of love; it requires time spent making and ripening the cheese.
Despite this, it is well worth doing, as cutting into your very own
homemade hard cheese is fantastic. After all those months of
maturing, all the flavours you are tasting are down to the hard
work and time you have put into it.

When making hard cheese, you will learn some fantastic
cheesemaking skills. Affinage is also important for hard cheese, so
you will further develop this skill. And you will learn the unique art
of Cheddaring. After curds form during the cheesemaking process,
they are cut into smaller pieces to get rid of the whey. The smaller
the curds are cut, the more liquid will drain from them and the
firmer the cheese will be. This process is used when making almost
all types of cheese, but is taken one step further for Cheddar.

For Cheddar, the curds are cut, then pressed together into slabs.
The slabs of curds are stacked on top of each other and the weight
of stacking presses out even more moisture. Then the slabs are
cut again, pressed into slabs once more and restacked. This is
Cheddaring, and it results in a cheese with a crumbly, layered,
dense texture.

As ever, keep a note of each stage of your cheesemaking, so you can
change and adjust the recipe as you practise.

Mature Comté (right) is full of crystals and is crunchy, with a strong and sharp aftertaste. Just a small chunk will give you a burst of long-lasting flavour. This cheese has been matured for 36 to 42 months and is sweet with a nutty flavour. A most exceptional Comté.

Ossau-Iraty (left) is my favourite cheese of all time. With a drizzle of truffle honey, this is the best thing you will ever taste. Beneath its amber, mould-dappled rind lies an ivory paste that is both slightly gritty and very rich, boasting grassy-sweet and nutty flavours.

Cornish Yarg (front) is a delicate, buttery cheese, which is wrapped in nettle leaves. It tends to have a fluffy-textured centre with lactic flavours and a buttery, creamy body underneath a beautiful rich green earthy rind.

Cheddar

I was lucky enough to be raised on good farmhouse Cheddar, and it is still one of my favourite cheeses. I love a good British Cheddar like Westcombe, Quicke's or Montgomery's, and have found inspiration for this recipe from those traditional makers.

9 litres (15¾ pints/38 cups) milk

⅛ tsp calcium chloride, diluted in 50ml (1¾fl oz) water

⅛ tsp mesophilic culture

½ tsp liquid rennet

2 tbsp salt

cheese wax (optional)

MAKES 800g (1lb 12oz)

You will need: cheesecloth or muslin sheets, an instant-read thermometer, a curd knife and a Cheddar mould

1 In a large saucepan, heat the milk to 29°C (85°F), stirring frequently to prevent it sticking to the bottom of the pan. As the milk is heating up, add the calcium chloride. When the milk reaches the required temperature, add the mesophilic culture, stir, cover with the pan lid and set aside for 1 hour.

2 Stir the milk, then add the rennet. Mix in thoroughly to make sure the rennet is evenly distributed, then set the milk aside for another hour until you see the curds separate from the whey.

3 Using a curd knife, carefully cut the curds into 6mm (¼-inch) cubes and leave them to rest for 5 minutes.

4 Return the curds to the heat and slowly heat to 38°C (100°F), for about 30 minutes. Once the curds reach 38°C (100°F), maintain the temperature for a further 30 minutes, stirring continuously.

5 Remove from the heat and leave the curds to settle at the bottom of the saucepan; this should take about 30 minutes.

6 Line a sieve (fine-mesh strainer) with cheesecloth or muslin and set it over a pan. Carefully spoon your curds into the strainer and leave them to drain for 15 minutes. Remove the whey from the pan, place into a separate bowl and set aside.

7 Transfer the curds to a chopping (cutting) board. They should be jelly-like in consistency. Cut the curds into five slices, return to the pan and cover with a lid.

4

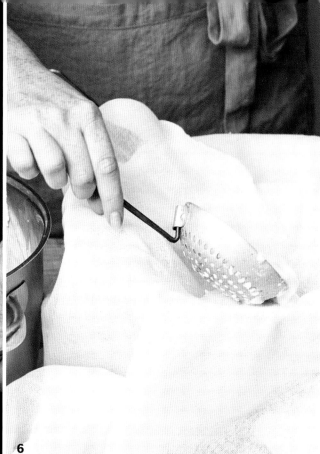

6

8   Fill your sink with water at a temperature of
    39°C (102°F) and place the pan of curds into it,
    keeping the temperature of the curds about 38°C
    (100°F). Turn the stacked curd slices every 15
    minutes for 2 hours; this is Cheddaring.

9   After 2 hours the curds will be shiny and firm.
    Remove from the pan and cut into 1.25cm (½-
    inch) cubes. Return to the pan, cover with
    the lid and place in the sink filled with 39°C
    (102°F) water.

10 After 10 minutes, stir the curds with your
    fingers. Then do this two more times, leaving 10
    minutes between each stirring.

11 Remove the pan from the sink and add the salt,
    stirring it through gently.

12 Line the mould with a cheesecloth or muslin
    sheet. Carefully add the curds, wrapping the
    cloth around the cheese and holding down with
    5kg (11lb) of weight for 20 minutes.

12

13 Remove the weights from the cheese, unwrap and flip the cheese over. Rewrap using a fresh piece of cloth. Now press the cheese with 18kg (40lb) of weight for 12 hours.

14 Remove the weights from the cheese again and repeat – unwrap and flip the cheese, rewrap and this time press the cheese with 23kg (50lb) of weight for 24 hours. Remove the cheese and leave it to air dry, uncovered, for 2 days, until it is smooth to touch.

15 Now is time to wax your cheese, if you would like to. Waxing cheese protects hard cheese from airborne bacteria, unwanted mould and drying out. It is typically used for cheeses that are going to be aged for a couple of months or so, while cheeses that will be matured for over 5 months are usually cloth-wrapped. I use a prepared wax, so no need to heat, just empty it into a deep bowl, then hold one side of the cheese and dip it into the melted wax, holding it there for only about 3 seconds. Place the waxed cheese onto some greaseproof (wax) paper and leave it to harden for about 1 hour, then move it to a wire (cooling) rack set over a plate. Pour a second coat of wax over for a smooth finish and leave to harden once more.

16 Alternatively, keep your cheese in a cloth (see page 142). Whether waxed or wrapped, you can mature the cheese at a temperature of 10–15°C (50–60°F) for 60 days. The longer you leave it, the more mature it will become.

Mature Clothbound Cheddar

Wrapping your cheese in cheesecloth is a great way to add a wonderful rind, amazing flavours and beautiful textures to the cheese. I use it a lot on Cheddars, because they lend themselves so well to this ripening technique.

Lay out enough cheesecloth or muslin to cover a whole cheese. Rub the Cheddar in oil, butter or lard, making sure you fully coat the cheese and create an even layer. Wrap the cheese fully in the cloth, pressing it into the cheese, using the fat to keep it in place. Repeat once more with more fat and cloth. Once done, place the cloth-wrapped cheese in a cool, dry place away from draughts and sunlight for the duration of the ageing period. The technique stops unwanted mould from growing directly on the rind of the cheese; instead, the mould grows on the cheesecloth, allowing the cheese to develop flavours undisturbed. To test, unwrap the cheese, then use a cheese iron (like a cheese apple corer) to extract a small sample from the centre of the uncut cheese wheel. Turn it around twice and pull it back slowly. After you have tasted the cheese, push the little plug back into the hole and seal with a little bit of fat.

4 tbsp brown ale

1 tsp English mustard powder

30g (1oz) butter

1 tsp Worcestershire sauce

100g (3½oz) Cheddar (see page 138), grated

100g (3½oz) Red Leicester (see page 150), grated

1 tbsp double (heavy) cream

2 thick slices of farmhouse bread

2 egg yolks

salt and freshly ground black pepper

SERVES 2

Welsh Rarebit

Welsh rarebit is perhaps the most famous Welsh dish of all, yet there is no evidence that it actually originated in Wales, although the Welsh have always had a reputation for loving it. Wherever this dish started out, it is the most delicious cheesy treat and there is nothing better on a rainy day. I always love it with pickle for extra relish.

In a pan, combine a little of the brown ale with the mustard powder to make a paste. Add the rest of the ale, the butter and Worcestershire sauce and place the pan over a medium heat until the butter has melted.

Add the Cheddar and Red Leicester and stir until melted and smooth. Add a pinch of salt and pepper and the cream, then set aside to cool.

Preheat the grill (broiler) to medium and toast the bread on both sides.

Stir the egg yolks into the cheese mixture until smooth, then spoon the mixture onto the toast slices and return to the grill (broiler) until golden and bubbling.

STAR CHEESEMAKER
QUICKE'S, UK

Cheese: Vintage Clothbound Cheddar

The 1,500-acre Quicke family farm is located near Newton St Cyres in Devon and has been farmed by the family for over 400 years. Now the wonderful Mary Quicke, the 14th generation, runs the dairy. Mary's passion for her herd and artisan methods make her a leading authority on traditional cheese production. Since the age of 19, when I started in the cheese industry, I have looked up to Mary, as a wonderful role model and a real inspiration for women in cheese. Not forgetting that these are the best Cheddars around; after making clothbound cheese for five generations, Quicke's flavour profiles capture the best of the grass, soil and seasons.

Cheddar and Veggie Frittata

This is Malcolm McGlynn's famous veggie frittata recipe . . . in our household anyway. My dad has been making this since I was a little girl and it's one of my favourite dinners.

200g (7oz) waxy new potatoes, cut into quarters

100g (3½oz) asparagus, chopped

1 tbsp olive oil

1 red onion, thinly sliced

50g (1¾oz) cherry tomatoes, sliced

1 red (bell) pepper, deseeded and thinly sliced

6 eggs

50g (1¾oz) Cheddar (see page 138), grated

2 tbsp double (heavy) cream

salt and freshly ground black pepper

SERVES 4

Cook the new potatoes in a pan of boiling water for about 5 minutes until tender. Add the asparagus and continue to cook for 1 minute, then drain and leave to cool.

Heat the olive oil in a non-stick heatproof frying pan (skillet). Add the onion and cook until golden brown, then add the tomatoes and peppers and cook until softened.

Preheat the grill (broiler) to high.

In a jug (large measuring cup), mix the eggs, half the cheese, the cream and a pinch of salt and pepper. Pour the mixture over the onions, red (bell) pepper and tomatoes, then add the asparagus and potatoes.

Sprinkle over the remaining cheese and cook under the grill (broiler) for 5–10 minutes until golden and cooked through. Serve with lamb's lettuce.

Very Naughty Mac and Cheese

This is the ultimate mac and cheese – no holding back or counting calories here! It has a whopping five cheeses in it, and is a proper gooey, stringy mac and cheese.

400g (14oz) dried curly macaroni

550ml (19 fl oz/2¼ cups) milk

50g (1¾oz) salted butter

50g (1¾oz) plain (all-purpose) flour

50g (1¾oz) fontina, grated

40g (1½oz) Parmesan, grated

50g (1¾oz) mozzarella (see page 44), grated

275g (9¾oz) Cheddar (see page 138), grated

½ tsp mustard powder

50ml (1¾ fl oz) double (heavy) cream

25g (¾oz) raclette cheese, grated

salt

SERVES 4

Bring a large pan of salted water to the boil and cook the pasta until al dente. Drain in a colander and leave to stand for a few moments.

Meanwhile, place another pan over a medium heat and add the milk, then heat until hot, but not boiling.

In a third pan, add the butter and heat until melted, then reduce the heat and gradually stir in the flour using a wooden spoon until you have a paste. Continue to cook, stirring continuously, for 3–4 minutes until the roux turns golden in colour.

Add the hot milk to the roux little by little and continue to stir until the two are fully combined. Cook over a medium heat for a further 4 minutes until the mixture starts to thicken. Keep stirring to ensure the mixture doesn't stick to the bottom of the pan.

Stir in the fontina, Parmesan, half of the mozzarella and 250g (9oz) of the Cheddar. Add the mustard powder, cream and the drained pasta and stir to combine.

Preheat the grill (broiler) to high.

Transfer the mixture to a heatproof dish. Sprinkle the raclette cheese and the rest of the Cheddar and mozzarella over the top and grill (broil) until the cheese is bubbling away. Serve with a side salad.

STAR CHEESEMAKER
COWS CREAMERY, CANADA

Cheeses: Avonlea Clothbound Cheddar

Cows Creamery is located on Canada's east coast, in Charlottetown, the capital city of Prince Edward Island. Cheesemaker Scott Linkletter was inspired to begin making Cheddar-style cheeses after a visit to the Orkney Islands, north of Scotland, where he met and befriended a local cheesemaker. Scott started making the wonderful clothbound Cheddar, which has a crumbly texture with a beautifully creamy, smooth, melt-in-the-mouth taste.

Cheese and Garlic Scones

This is one of my favourites. I was taught this recipe by the wonderful Nigel Slater, who came to my house a few years ago, and we made cheese scones from off-cuts (scraps of cheese) from the shop. I use Cheddar in mine, but you can use any cheese you like, really.

50g (1¾oz) butter, plus a little extra for greasing
225g (8oz) self-raising (self-rising) flour, plus extra for dusting
pinch of salt
200g (7oz) Cheddar (see page 138), grated
1 garlic clove, crushed
6 tbsp chopped fresh chives
150ml (5 fl oz/scant ⅔ cup) milk, plus extra for brushing

MAKES 4 LARGE SCONES

Preheat the oven to 220°C (425°F/Gas Mark 7) and lightly grease a baking sheet.

Mix together the flour and salt in a bowl, then rub in the butter using your fingertips. Stir in the cheese, garlic and chives, followed by the milk, to form a soft dough.

Turn the dough onto a floured surface and knead very lightly. Pat out to a round 2cm (¾ inch) thick. Using a 5cm (2-inch) cutter, stamp out rounds and place on the baking sheet.

Brush the tops of the scones with milk, then bake for about 12–15 minutes until you see them rise and they are golden brown. Leave to cool before eating.

Red Leicester

Red Leicester is a hard cheese, normally coloured with annatto, and can be dark yellow to red in colour. This is where the name comes from. I love making Red Leicester, mainly because the colour is so wonderful. Once made it can be kept in the refrigerator for ages, or waxed. It's so delicious on a good ploughman's board. Similar to Cheddar, but much milder, it's great for kids or if you prefer a good mild hard cheese.

7.5 litres (13 pints/32 cups) milk

1 packet direct-set mesophilic starter

4 drops annatto food colouring, diluted in 120ml (4 fl oz/½ cup) cold water

½ tsp liquid rennet, diluted in 120ml (4 fl oz/½ cup) cold water

5 tbsp salt

cheese wax (optional)

MAKES 800g (1lb 12oz)

You will need: cheesecloth or muslin sheets, an instant-read thermometer, a curd knife and a cheese mould

1 In your largest saucepan, heat the milk to 29°C (85°F) using the water bath method – setting the pan into a sink filled with hot water – rather than over direct heat. When the milk reaches the required temperature, add the mesophilic starter, leave for 30 seconds, then stir through the milk. Use a spoon in an up and down movement to make sure it is evenly distributed. Cover the milk and leave for 1 hour, then remove from the sink.

2 Next, add the colouring, stirring well to mix it into the milk.

3 Return the pan to the sink and, keeping the milk at 29°C (85°F), add the rennet and stir it in for 1 minute. Cover and leave for a further hour, keeping the milk at 29°C (85°F) by adding more hot water as necessary. Do not remove the lid.

4 After the hour is up, slowly bring the temperature up to 35°C (95°F). Keep stirring to prevent the milk sticking to the pan. Keep the mixture at 35°C (95°F) for 30 minutes.

5 Line a sieve (fine-mesh strainer) with cheesecloth or muslin set over a bowl, add the curds and drain. You might find it easier to transfer them with a jug (large measuring cup). Leave to sit for about 30 minutes.

6 Place the curds on a board and cut them into six long strips. Place them onto a draining board, cover with a warm cloth, and turn the curds over every 15 minutes for a total of 1 hour. Try to keep the cloth warm too.

7 Transfer to a large bowl. Add 2 tablespoons of the salt then crumble the curds in your hands for 2 minutes.

2

2

5

7

8 Transfer the curds to a clean cheesecloth or muslin sheet, wrap them tightly and weigh them down for 30 minutes – you can use two wooden boards and a few heavy books.

9 Now wrap the cheese in the cheesecloth and place it into a cheese mould. Press the cheese for 2 hours with some weights, such as tin cans, placed on a plate on top of the cheese. Then rewrap the cheese in a fresh piece of cloth, flip it over and press for another 2 hours. Rewrap, flip and press with double the amount of weight for 24 hours.

10 Remove the cheese from the cloth. Rub and coat it in the rest of the salt, then leave to sit at room temperature for 2 days until dry.

8

11 Now you can wax the cheese (see page 141) or leave it with a natural rind. I mature my Red Leicester for about 12 weeks at 13°C (55°F), but you can mature it for as long as you like; I have aged it for up to 12 months, which results in a very strong, mature cheese (left).

Red Leicester, Cherry Tomato and Courgette (Zucchini) Tarts

These little tarts are wonderful served as appetizers at a party, especially at Christmas, or great to take cold on a picnic. It is such an easy recipe, and you can make them ahead of time and freeze them, as they reheat beautifully.

1 sheet of readymade shortcrust pastry (pie dough)

200g (7oz) assorted cherry tomatoes

olive oil, for frying

2 small courgettes (zucchini), sliced 1cm (½ inch) thick

½ red onion, thinly sliced

4 eggs

100ml (3½ fl oz/scant ½ cup) milk

30g (1oz) plain (all-purpose) flour

handful of fresh basil, chopped

½ tsp cayenne

½ tsp mustard powder

200g (7oz) red Leicester (see page 1500, grated

1 tsp paprika

1 tsp each salt and freshly ground black pepper

MAKES 4 TARTS

Preheat the oven to 180°C (350°F/Gas Mark 4).

Cut four circles from the pastry (dough), around 10cm (4 inches) in diameter. Line individual tart tins (pans) with the pastry (dough), line with baking (parchment) paper and baking beans (pie weights) and blind bake for 12–15 minutes until golden.

Wash and slice the tomatoes, then place on a plate lined with kitchen paper (paper towels) to drain.

Heat a little olive oil in a frying pan (skillet) over a medium heat. Add the courgette (zucchini) slices in a single layer, season with salt and pepper and cook until lightly browned. Transfer to a plate and add the onion to the hot pan. Cook for just a few minutes until lightly browned but still crunchy. Add the onions to the courgette (zucchini) and set aside.

In a medium bowl, combine the eggs, milk, flour, basil, cayenne, mustard powder, salt and pepper. Beat by hand until well blended, or make it super-easy and use a stick (immersion) blender.

Sprinkle the cheese in the bottom of the baked crusts. Layer half the tomatoes, courgettes (zucchini) and onions over the cheese. Gently pour the egg mixture over, and top with the remaining tomatoes, courgettes (zucchini) and onions.

Sprinkle with paprika and bake for 30 minutes, or until the egg mixture is set in the centre. Cover the tarts with foil during baking if the crusts brown too quickly.

Remove from the tins (pans) and leave the tarts to cool on a wire (cooling) rack for 10–15 minutes before serving. They may also be served at room temperature.

Gouda

Gouda is a beautiful caramel-sweet cheese, with a real depth of flavour. This Dutch classic is a wonderful hard cheese and really rewarding to make. It is advanced cheesemaking at its best. This Gouda is quite a mild, smooth cheese, but it really comes alive during the maturing process, so the longer you mature it the more flavour you will get, and you can mature the cheese for up to eight months.

7.5 litres (13 pints/32 cups) milk

1 packet direct-set mesophilic starter

½ tsp rennet, diluted in 50ml (1¾fl oz) cold water

500g (1lb 1¾oz) salt

1 tbsp calcium chloride

cheese wax

MAKES 1kg (2lb 3oz)

You will need: cheesecloth or muslin sheets, an instant-read thermometer, a curd knife and a cheese mould

1 In a large pan over a low heat, heat the milk to 32°C (90°F), stirring frequently to prevent it sticking to the bottom of the pan, then add the mesophilic starter and stir well until it is evenly distributed. Remove the milk from the heat, cover and let it sit undisturbed for 15 minutes.

2 Add the rennet and stir through for 2 minutes. Cover and set aside for 1 hour.

3 Using a curd knife, cut the curds into 1cm (½-inch) cubes. Cover and set aside for 15 minutes.

4 Drain off one-third of the whey, then add to the pan 2.5 litres (4½ pints/10½ cups) of water at a temperature of 82°C (180°F). The temperature of the curds should be 32°C (90°F). Let the curds sit for 10 minutes, then pour off the whey until the tops of the curds are visible. Add another panful of water at 79°C (175°F). The overall temperature of the curds should be 38°C (100°F) and should stay like this for 15 minutes. Stir the curds to avoid sticking, then leave them, covered, for a further 40 minutes. Line a sieve (fine-mesh strainer) with cheesecloth or muslin, set over a bowl, then pour in the curds and leave to drain.

5 Gather the cloth up into a bag, squeeze out any remaining liquid and press the curds together. Once the curds are matted, transfer them to a cloth-lined mould and apply about 1kg (2lb 3oz) of weight set on a plate on top of the cheese for 1 hour.

4

5

5

5

STAR CHEESEMAKER
WESTLAND, THE NETHERLANDS

Cheese: Old Amsterdam Gouda

One of the Netherlands' most famous Goudas and a bestseller in my cheese shop, Old Amsterdam was first created in the 1940s by Lambert Westland and his family. Lambert's father, Gijsbert Westland, had originally been a fish merchant, but he had always had a passion for cheese, and soon became a cheesemonger, wholesaler and sold door to door. Today, Old Amsterdam is made at several Dutch dairies that work with high-quality milk, to the original family recipe. Old Amsterdam is the best-selling Gouda in the world, with rich, sweet flavours and a slightly caramel nutty bite.

6

6 Remove the weight, take the cheese out of the mould, unwrap it and flip it over. Rewrap it in a clean cloth and return it to the mould. Repeat every 15 minutes for 1 hour, then increase the weight by 500g (1lb 1¾oz) and press for a further 15 hours.

7 Make a brine mix. In a bowl, add the salt and calcium chloride to 3 litres (5¼ pints/12½ cups) of cold water. Unwrap the cheese and cover it completely in the brine. Leave it to soak for 10–12 hours, flipping it every couple of hours.

8 Remove the cheese from the brine and leave it to dry for 3 days in a cool, dry place.

9 Wax your cheese (see page 141), then leave it to mature in a cool, dark place for 4–6 months. For a more mature cheese, leave it for 9–12 months.

Gouda, Parmesan and Spinach Rolls

These are nice, strong-flavoured vegetarian rolls. Great as finger food at a party, or baked in a big batch to fill lunch boxes.

butter, for greasing

300g (10½oz) spinach, cooked and drained

8 tbsp Parmesan cheese, grated

250g (9oz) feta (see page 126), crumbled

1 onion, chopped

250g (9oz) mature Gouda (see page 156), grated

splash of milk

1 sheet of readymade puff pastry

2 eggs, beaten

MAKES 3 ROLLS

Preheat the oven to 200°C (400°F/Gas Mark 6) and grease a baking sheet.

In a large bowl, mix together all the ingredients except the pastry and eggs.

Unroll the pastry sheet and cut it lengthways into three equal pieces. Divide the cheese mixture into three and place one-third down the middle of each length of pastry dough.

Brush down one side of the dough with the beaten egg. Roll the dough around the cheese mix, using a little of the egg mixture to seal the edges. Place in the refrigerator for 20 minutes.

Brush the tops of the rolls with the rest of the egg mixture. Bake for 20 minutes, or until golden and cooked through.

STAR CHEESEMAKER
CORNISH GOUDA COMPANY, UK

Cheeses: Mature Gouda, Flavoured Gouda

Giel Spierings founded the Cornish Gouda Company, a small farm-based business near Looe, Cornwall. In an attempt to save his family's dairy farm by diversifying the business, Giel went to the Netherlands to learn how to make cheese. He came back to Cornwall and started practising. The results were good – he started winning awards and there was great interest from many quarters in selling his hand-produced cheeses. The company now also offer a range of different flavoured cheeses, including some limited edition ones.

Classic Croque Monsieur

Croque monsieur is the gourmet French version of a toasted ham and cheese sandwich – and it is delicious!

100g (3½oz) unsalted butter, plus 1 tbsp for frying

2 tbsp plain (all-purpose) flour

250ml (9 fl oz/1 cup) warm milk

pinch of nutmeg

pinch of freshly ground black pepper

2 thick slices of sourdough bread

2 tsp Dijon mustard

300g (10½oz) Gruyère

150g (5oz) thickly sliced ham

SERVES 1

To make a béchamel sauce, melt the butter in a pan over a medium heat. Once melted, add the flour, stirring continuously to make sure it doesn't burn. Add the warm milk gradually and stir until smooth and thickened, then add the nutmeg and pepper and set aside.

Spread one side of each slice of bread with the mustard. Slice 200g (7oz) of the Gruyère, then top one slice of bread with the ham and sliced cheese. Place the pieces of bread together to make a sandwich.

In a large pan, melt 1 tablespoon butter, add the sandwich and lightly cook on both sides.

Preheat the grill (broiler) and line a baking sheet with a piece of non-stick baking (parchment) paper. Transfer the sandwich to the baking sheet. Grate the remaining Gruyère, then top the sandwich with the béchamel sauce and grated cheese. Cook under the grill (broiler) until golden brown and bubbling.

Cheese Fondue

The French word 'fondue' (melted) describes a very old traditional method of spearing bread cubes onto a long fork and dipping them into melted cheese. It was invented to use up stale bread, and both the Swiss and French would originally eat this dish in the winter months because it was delicious but also warming. This is the perfect dish to enjoy with family and friends.

200g (7oz) Emmental, grated

200g (7oz) Gruyère, grated

50g (1¾oz) Appenzeller, grated

3 tbsp plain (all-purpose) flour

1 garlic clove, halved

250ml (9 fl oz/1 cup) white wine

1 tsp lemon juice

2 tbsp Kirsch

pinch of freshly ground black pepper

pinch of nutmeg

SERVES 2

Put all the grated cheese in a large bowl and add the flour.

Rub the fondue pot or a saucepan with the halves of garlic. Add the wine and heat gently, but do not boil. Add the lemon juice and the Kirsch.

Slowly add the cheeses, stirring continuously until the cheese has the texture of a smooth sauce. Add the pepper and nutmeg, then serve with cubes of crusty bread for dipping.

STAR CHEESEMAKER
AFFINEUR WALO, SWITZERLAND

Cheeses: Gruyère, Vacherin, Raclette

Walo von Mühlenen is the fifth generation of cheese maturers in his family, whose cheese history dates back to 1867. His technique is to source raw milk cheese from the very best farms. Then he selects only the best cheeses. These are then nurtured for up to 18 months in special cellars, with optimal conditions and cultures built up over time. It is not surprising that Walo has won World Champion cheese for his Gruyère no fewer than five times. Walo's cellars are in the canton of Fribourg, the heart of Swiss cheesemaking.

Tortellini Bake

This recipe was born when I didn't have the energy or time to make mac and cheese. It's a super-quick, easy dish, and a great alternative to the original classic. I also make it using gnocchi.

100g (3½oz) butter, plus extra for greasing

50g (1¾oz) plain (all-purpose) flour

550ml (19 fl oz/2¼ cups) milk

1 tsp Dijon mustard

pinch of nutmeg

1 garlic clove, crushed

100g (3½oz) fontina, grated

250g (9oz) pack of tortellini (the flavour of your choice)

3 smoked streaky (lean) bacon slices, cooked and chopped

150g (5oz) Cheddar (see page 138), grated

50g (1¾oz) Parmesan, grated

salt and freshly ground black pepper

SERVES 2

Preheat the oven to 200°C (400°F/Gas Mark 6) and grease 2 baking dishes with butter.

Melt the butter in a saucepan over a medium heat, then add the flour and stir through. Cook over a low heat until a paste forms, then add the milk gradually. Stir the sauce and simmer for a minute or two until it thickens. Add the mustard, nutmeg, crushed garlic and the grated fontina. Stir through, then set aside.

Cook the tortellini following the directions on the packet.

Drain the pasta, then stir into the cheese sauce with the cooked bacon. Pour the pasta into the baking dishes and top with the Cheddar and Parmesan. Bake for 25 minutes until the cheese is melted and golden brown. Remove from the oven, leave to cool slightly then serve.

Aligot

Aligot is a magical cheesy mashed potato. This is a French recipe from the Pyrenees, which blends potatoes and cheese and is traditionally served alongside meat. If you love mashed potatoes and cheese, this is the recipe for you.

1.5kg (3lb 5oz) potatoes

250g (9oz) unsalted butter

350ml (12 fl oz/1½ cups) double (heavy) cream

900g (2lb) Gruyère, grated

450g (1lb) mozzarella (see page 44), grated

salt and freshly ground black pepper

SERVES 4

Peel the potatoes and cut into 2.5cm (1-inch) cubes. Place the potatoes into a large pan of boiling water with a pinch of salt. Cover and cook until tender, about 10–15 minutes.

Drain the potatoes and leave to cool for 5 minutes. Pulse the cooked potatoes in a food processor until you have a fine purée. Return to the large pan with the butter, cream and a pinch of salt and the pepper. Stir thoroughly to combine.

Add the grated Gruyère and mozzarella and mix into the potatoes with a wooden spoon; put a bit of elbow grease into it, as you are looking for the cheese and potatoes to come together and have a stringy, elastic texture. Season to taste, then serve.

Comté, Ham and Onion Sunday Brunch Rolls

Sunday brunch is the best meal of the week, and I love spending it with some of my favourite people: Tim, Simon, Charlie, Mike, Alice and Mel. Brunch is such a luxury and an easy way to enjoy a lazy weekend. My Sunday brunch roll is the best – ideal for one or make lots to share with friends.

4 crusty rolls

5 eggs

300g (10½oz) ham, chopped

2 onions, finely chopped

400g (14oz) Comté, grated

SERVES 4

Preheat the oven to 190°C (375°F/Gas Mark 5).

Start with the rolls: cut 4cm (1½ inches) across the length of the bread; then hollow out the inside, making sure to leave a thick shell. Place the rolls on a piece of non-stick baking (parchment) paper on a baking sheet.

In a bowl, mix together 1 of the eggs, the ham, onions and Comté, then fill your rolls with the mixture. Break the remaining eggs on top and bake for 15–20 minutes until golden brown. Serve hot.

Butternut Squash Soup with Comté

Quick and easy, creamy and comforting, this soup has the perfect blend of butternut squash and Comté. The cheese brings a lovely nuttiness to the soup, making this perfect on a chilly evening.

1 onion, chopped

20g (¾oz) butter

400g (14oz) butternut squash, peeled and cut into cubes

200g (7oz) potato, peeled and cut into cubes

500ml (18 fl oz/2 cups) hot chicken stock

150ml (5 fl oz/scant ⅔ cup) double (heavy) cream

200g (7oz) Comté, diced

pinch of salt, freshly ground black pepper and nutmeg

dried chill flakes, to serve

SERVES 4

In a large saucepan, sweat the onion in the butter over a medium heat for 3 minutes. Add the squash and potato and cook for another 3 minutes. Add the chicken stock and simmer, covered, for 15 minutes.

Once the potatoes and squash are cooked through, add the Comté and the cream, reserving 1 tbsp for serving. Heat through for 2 minutes, then transfer to a food processor and blend to a smooth soup.

Add the salt, pepper and nutmeg, then serve in individual bowls, with the remaining cream drizzled over the top, and the dried chilli flakes sprinkled over.

Jalapeño and Parmesan Crisps

A great go-to snack, Parmesan crisps are so easy and quick to make. I always like to have them on standby, just in case I fancy a nibble. Serve with some yoghurt for dipping.

150g (5oz) Parmesan, grated

2 medium jalapeño chillies, thinly sliced (or use Scotch bonnet chillies if you like things a little spicier)

100g (3½oz) provolone, grated

MAKES 8 CRISPS

Preheat the oven to 180°C (350°F/Gas Mark 4).

On a piece of non-stick baking (parchment) paper, make eight mountains of Parmesan (about 1 tablespoon each), about 5cm (2 inches) apart.

Lay the jalapeño slices on a baking sheet and cook for 5 minutes. Remove from the oven and increase the temperature to 220°C (425°F/Gas Mark 7).

Once the jalapeños are cooked, place them on top of the Parmesan mountains, pressing them down into the cheese.

Split the provolone into eight and spread on top of the jalapeños and Parmesan. Cook for 10 minutes until golden and crisp. Once cooled, remove carefully with a palette knife. Serve immediately.

Blue Cheese

Blue Cheese

You either love or hate blue cheese – there is no in-between – and I am a lover. Not only do I love the taste, I love the story of how blue cheese was apparently invented. There are a few different versions of the story, including that it was invented by accident when a drunken cheesemaker left behind a half-eaten loaf of bread in a moist cheese cave. Or by the French shepherd, who left his cheese in a cave while he was in pursuit of the love of his life.

Not only is blue cheese wonderfully delicious, but scientists have discovered that the cheese, known for its mould and blue veins, has specific anti-inflammatory properties – which could explain why the French enjoy such good health despite favouring a diet high in saturated fat. The properties of blue cheese, which is traditionally aged in caves in the South of France, were found to work best in acidic environments of the body, such as the lining of the stomach or the surface of the skin. So cheese is actually really good for you . . . an even better excuse to make and eat loads!

Blue cheese is a generic term used to describe a cheese produced with cow's milk, sheep's milk or goat's milk, and ripened with cultures of the mould Penicillium. Blue cheese has distinct blue veins, which give it its name and, often, an assertive flavour. The moulds range from pale green to dark blue, and may be accompanied by white and crusty brown moulds. These veins are created during its production, when the cheese is 'spiked' with stainless steel rods to let oxygen circulate and encourage the growth of the mould. This process also softens the texture and develops the distinctive 'blue' flavour.

So here is how you can make your very own blue cheese at home, and some recipes using your homemade blue.

Shropshire blue (left) is a full-flavoured, bright orange blue cheese that is hard to miss. It tastes fabulous, with its smooth texture and sharp, tangy taste.

Morgan's homemade blue (front) is matured at home – and very yummy, if I say so myself.

Spanish Cabrales (right) is famous for being one of the strongest blue cheeses made. This will numb your gums. The texture and mouth feel is drier than many other blue cheeses, and the sensation is intense.

Blue Cheese

So . . . blue cheese. Homemade blue is fabulous, but even experienced home cooks are hesitant to try making it. The main ingredients are deceptively basic: milk, culture, rennet. Then comes the Penicillium mould, which can seem scary, but once you have this recipe down the rewards are worth it. Nothing beats it!

7.5 litres (13 pints/32 cups) milk

½ tsp calcium chloride, dissolved in 60ml (2 fl oz/¼ cup) cold water

¼ tsp Penicillium roqueforti (blue mould)

½ tsp MM100 mesophilic culture

1 tsp rennet, dissolved in 4 tsp cooled boiled water

500g (1lb 1¾oz) salt

MAKES 250g (9oz)

You will need: a cheesecloth or muslin sheet, an instant-read thermometer, a curd knife, draining mat and a round cheese mould

1 In a large pan over a low heat, slowly warm the milk to 32°C (90°F), stirring continuously. When it reaches the required temperature, add the Penicillium roqueforti, the MM100 culture and the diluted calcium chloride. Mix in well, using an across and up and down motion. Remove from the heat, cover and leave undisturbed for 1 hour.

2 Stir in the dissolved rennet, again in an across, up and down movement, to make sure it is mixed in well. Cover and leave for another hour.

3 At this point you should see the curds separate and float on top. Cut the curds into 3cm (1¼-inch) cubes, then leave to stand for 10–15 minutes.

4 For the next hour, stir the curds gently every 5–10 minutes. After 1 hour, cover and let the curds sit, undisturbed, for 10 minutes.

5 Line a sieve (fine-mesh strainer) with cheesecloth or muslin and set it over a large bowl. Carefully pour or ladle the cheese curds in and leave for 10 minutes to allow all the whey to drain away.

6 Add 3 tablespoons of the salt and mix well, then leave in the bowl for 5 minutes to rest. If you feel the curds they should have a firm texture. Gather the cloth into a bag and squeeze to get rid of all the whey, then return the curds to the strainer in the cloth.

1

3

5

6

7 Place a round cheese mould on a plate; you can make one large cheese or a few smaller ones, depending on the moulds you have. Fill the cheese mould nearly to the top using a slotted spoon, leaving a little space. Set aside for 15 minutes, then come back to the cheese and turn, placing a board below and on top of the cheese mould. Holding both boards firmly, you should be able to flip it over in one movement. Continue to flip the cheese every 15 minutes for 3 hours. On the final flip, make sure the cheese mould is standing upright and leave the cheese to drain overnight, covered.

8 The next day, remove the cheese from the mould, place on a shallow plate and lightly sprinkle 5 tablespoons of salt all over the cheese, making sure you cover every surface. Shake off any excess salt and leave the cheese to stand for 4 days, ideally somewhere with high humidity, at about 15°C (59°F). Each day, re-salt and turn the cheese.

9 After 4 days it is time to spike the cheese. I use the end of my thermometer for this, but any spiked object will do. Poke the cheese every couple of centimetres (1 inch) apart. This allows the mould to start growing.

10 Place some kitchen paper (paper towels) and a sushi or plastic mat in a container, then place your cheese on top. Do not fully close the lid, and place in a cool environment of 10°C (50°F) for about 1 month. Be sure to turn the cheese once a week so all the moisture doesn't gather at the bottom. Change the paper weekly, too.

11 Once the month is up, there will be mould on the outside of the cheese. Scrape this off with a knife and leave for a further month, then repeat the process one more time. Give the cheese a total of 3 months maturing.

12 Now you can wrap your cheese in foil, nice and tight to make sure there isn't any exposure. Place the cheese in the refrigerator and mature for a further 2 months. Be sure to turn the cheese every 2 weeks.

13 After this the cheese will be ready to eat. It will be a mild blue, but for a stronger cheese you can keep maturing it in the refrigerator for a further 6 months.

Matured blue cheese at 4 weeks (left)
and 9 weeks (right).

STAR CHEESEMAKER
FORMATGES CAMPS, SPAIN

Cheese: Blau del Nèt Blue

Spanish brothers Toni and Robert Camps
founded Formatges Camps in 2000 in Lleida,
Spain, to diversify their family's agricultural
business, focusing on the artisanal
production of sheep and goat cheeses.
Today the company makes 12 different
cheeses, my favourite being the Blau del Nèt;
this cave-matured blue cheese is buttery and
rich with a creamy bite, yet it is slightly spicy.
The brothers were among the first to produce
blue cheeses in the region of Catalonia, and
now their wonderful cheeses have really
made their mark.

Baked Eggs with Blue Cheese

This easy weekend treat can be tweaked, adding tomatoes, bacon or whatever you fancy. Serve with toast for dipping.

20g (¾oz) salted butter, for greasing

400g (14oz) spinach, chopped

2 slices of good-quality ham, chopped

250g (9oz) blue cheese (see page 178), chopped

200ml (7 fl ox/generous ¾ cup) single (light) cream

2 eggs

salt and freshly ground black pepper

SERVES 2

Preheat the oven to 240°C (475°F/Gas Mark 9). Lightly grease an ovenproof frying pan (skillet) with the butter.

Place the spinach, ham and cheese in the pan, then add the cream. Crack the eggs on top and season with salt and pepper.

Place in the hot oven for 8–10 minutes, or until the whites are set but the yolks are still runny, then serve straight away.

STAR CHEESEMAKER
COLSTON BASSETT DAIRY, UK

Cheeses: Blue Stilton, Shropshire Blue

Colston Bassett lies near the Nottinghamshire–Leicestershire border, in an area known as the Vale of Belvoir. Many villages in this area had small Stilton dairies in the 19th century, most of which have now disappeared. For over 100 years, Colston Bassett Dairy has been making the finest-quality Blue Stilton, 'King of Cheeses', and in my eyes the best blue cheese money can buy. Colston Bassett's highly skilled cheesemakers follow the same time-honoured recipe and methods used by generations to make this unique, award-winning cheese, taking milk from the same pastures and farms that founded the dairy as a co-operative in 1913.

STAR CHEESEMAKER
ROQUEFORT PAPILLON, FRANCE

Cheese: Roquefort Papillon

As I have mentioned, my favourite story of the origin of a cheese is the young shepherd, in love with a shepherdess, leaving his rye bread and sheep's cheese in a cave to pursue the girl, and returning to discover his meal covered in a blue-green mould. Today, rye bread forms an integral part of the manufacture of Roquefort Papillon, the world's most famous Roquefort. It is in its crumb that the Penicillium roqueforti develops, the fungus that gives the cheese its taste and its green and blue marbling. To preserve the tradition and entirely control the production, they stick to the original recipe.

Blue Cheese Tarte Tatin

This is a dish I came up with a few years ago for a New Year's Eve party. I was going to make a traditional sweet tarte tatin, but decided to attempt a savoury version instead. And the result was this delicious recipe, perfect for sharing.

15 cherry tomatoes

50g (1¾oz) sundried tomatoes

250g (9oz) creamy blue cheese (see page 178)

1 tsp herbes de Provence

150g (5oz) piquillo peppers, chopped

100g (3½oz) black olives, pitted

handful of fresh chives, chopped

8 fresh basil leaves

1 tbsp thick balsamic vinegar

2 tbsp olive oil

1 sheet of readymade puff pastry

2 tbsp honey

50g (1¾oz) pine nuts

salt and freshly ground black pepper

SERVES 2

Preheat the oven to 200°C (400°F/Gas Mark 6).

Place all the ingredients except the pastry dough, honey and pine nuts into a large square baking dish. Season with salt and pepper, then lay the pastry sheet over the filling, tucking in the edges. Bake for 35–40 minutes until the pastry is crispy and golden.

Leave to cool in the dish for 5 minutes, then place a flat board over the dish and flip it over. Drizzle with a little honey and sprinkle over the pine nuts, then cut into pieces and serve with lamb's lettuce.

Cheesemonger Tips

Flavouring Cheese

Now you have had a go at making your own cheese, you can carry on experimenting, adding a little more or a little less of certain things. I love to experiment with the cheeses I've made, and one of the ways I do this is to flavour them in different ways. Here are some ideas, but let your imagination run wild – above all, experiment and have fun!

Yoghurt Cheese

1kg (2lb 3oz) natural (plain) yoghurt

1 tsp salt

handful of dried thyme, leaves only, finely chopped

½ tsp crushed black pepper

extra-virgin olive oil, for preserving

fresh thyme sprigs, for preserving

MAKES 250g (9oz)

1 Place the yoghurt, salt, thyme and pepper in a large bowl, then stir together.

2 Scoop the mix into a double layer of cheesecloth or muslin set over a bowl. Following the steps on pages 24–25, create a cloth bag and hang the yoghurt above the bowl and leave to drain overnight.

3 Discard the whey in the bowl below. Unwrap the cloth bag, slightly oil your hands and roll the cheese mixture into small balls. Place the cheese balls into a clean, sterilized jar with a few thyme sprigs, cover with olive oil and seal. This will preserve the cheese and it can be kept for up to 2 weeks in the refrigerator.

Camembert

Camembert is delicious and you can do so much with it – and it's also full of history.

Legend has it that the invention of what would become the most famous of all French cheeses is attributed to Marie Harel, who is reputed to have created the first Camembert in 1791 in the small village of Camembert in the Orne, during the French Revolution, after listening to advice from a refractory priest from Brie. This new cheese soon became more widely known thanks to the opening of the railway line between Paris and Normandy in 1850; then, in 1860, came the invention of the wooden box, which would enable the cheese to be transported more easily and go on to conquer the rest of the world!

The famous poplar-wood box, now mandatory, revolutionized the transport and commercialization of this cheese, but the label affixed to its lid also contributed to its success, adding a touch of soul and telling a story.

And yes, Camembert is a real treat, but believe it or not there are health benefits, too. Foods produced via fermentation, like Camembert, are renowned for their probiotic properties. Camembert is simply full of them! It also has a much lower fat content than other cheeses, at only 21 per cent. But undoubtedly the most important attribute of Camembert is that it is good for the soul.

Camembert facts

- It takes 2.2 litres (4 pints/9½ cups) of milk to produce one Camembert.
- France exports around 30,000 tonnes (metric tons) of Camembert per year.
- It takes 5 ladlefuls of curds to produce one Camembert de Normandie AOP.
- 30–35 days of maturing are required to produce a cheese that is mature in the middle.

See pages 192–96 for some of the best ways to flavour Camembert.

STAR CHEESEMAKER
FROMAGERIE GRAINDORGE, FRANCE

Cheeses: Camembert, Neufchâtel, Livarot, Pont l'Evêque

Situated in the heart of Normandy in the Pays d'Auge since 1910, the company specializes in the production of the four Norman Protected Designations of Origin (PDO) cheeses: Livarot, Pont-l'Evêque, Camembert de Normandie, and Neufchâtel. Their methods may have changed, but the spirit still remains: tradition, simplicity and indulgence are values that have passed through the generations and are still alive and well today among the men and women who make my favourite cheeses. Hooray for you, Graindorge.

The Classic Baked Camembert

A lovely gooey baked Camembert is a timeless classic. It never fails to impress, served with loads of crusty bread for dipping. The best type of comfort food with minimal effort. Ideal!

1 x 250g (9oz) wheel of Camembert in a box

1 garlic clove, sliced

3–4 sprigs of fresh rosemary

1 tsp olive oil

a splash of white wine

Preheat the oven to 200°C (400°F/Gas Mark 6). Remove the Camembert from the box and unwrap it, then put the cheese back in the bottom half of the box, leaving the lid off.

Pierce the top of the cheese in several places with a sharp knife and insert pieces of garlic and sprigs of rosemary into the slits. Drizzle the cheese with olive oil and a splash of white wine.

Place on a baking sheet and bake for 10 minutes, or until you see the cheese bubble.

My Dreamy Baked Vacherin

Vacherin mont d'or is perhaps one of the most sought-after cheeses on the market come September. When this cheese comes into season, it means winter is on the way, so there is no better way to eat it than baked, next to an open fire. Heaven!

1 x 450g (1lb) vacherin mont d'or in a box

3 shallots, finely chopped

2 garlic cloves, crushed

20g (¾oz) butter

2 sprigs of fresh rosemary, finely chopped

scant 2 tbsp white wine

(illustrated on page 195, top left)

Preheat the oven to 180°C (350°F/Gas Mark 4). Get your vacherin ready by unwrapping it and cutting the top off the cheese with a sharp knife. Put the cheese back in its box.

In a pan, cook the shallots and garlic in the butter until soft. Add the rosemary and white wine, then cook off the alcohol for a few minutes. Set aside to rest for 10 minutes.

Spread a thin layer of cooked shallots over the cheese, cutting down into the cheese so the mixture goes all the way through.

Place the wooden lid back on the cheese and wrap the box in foil. Place on baking sheet and bake for 10 minutes.

Camembert with Calvados

2 slices of stale bread, crusts removed

2 tbsp Calvados (apple brandy)

1 x 250g (9oz) wheel of Camembert, semi-ripe (this will absorb the alcohol better)

(illustrated opposite, top right)

Preheat the oven to 180°C (350°F/Gas Mark 4). Place the bread on a baking sheet and bake for 3–4 minutes, then remove from the oven and crush with a rolling pin until you have fine crumbs.

Pour the Calvados into a bowl. With a knife, remove the entire rind of the Camembert, then place the cheese in the Calvados, making sure the whole cheese is covered. Leave for 30 minutes, then carefully turn and leave for another 30 minutes.

Push the cheese into the crumb mixture, moving it around until evenly coated. Set aside for 1 hour before serving.

Parma-Ham-Wrapped Baked Camembert

handful of fresh chives

1 x 250g (9oz) wheel of Camembert

10 slices of Parma ham

(illustrated opposite, bottom left)

Preheat the oven to 200°C (400°F/Gas Mark 6). Line a baking sheet with non-stick baking (parchment) paper.

Arrange half the chives on top of the Camembert. Place 5 slices of Parma ham over the chives.

Carefully turn the Camembert over and fold in the ends of the Parma slices to enclose, then repeat with the remaining chives and Parma ham on this side to completely enclose the Camembert.

Place the Camembert on the lined sheet. Bake for 15 minutes, or until the Parma ham is crisp and the Camembert is soft. Transfer to a serving platter and serve with toasted bread.

Mushroom, Garlic and Truffle Baked Camembert

1 x 250g (9oz) wheel of Camembert in a box

1 tbsp truffle oil

handful of chestnut (cremini) mushrooms

1 shallot, finely chopped

1 garlic clove, crushed

2 tbsp chopped fresh parsley

2 sage leaves

salt and freshly ground black pepper

(illustrated opposite, bottom right)

Preheat the oven to 250°C (475°F/Gas Mark 9).

Remove the Camembert from the box and unwrap it. Put the cheese back in the bottom half of the box, leaving the lid off, and set it on a baking sheet. Bake for about 10 minutes until soft.

Meanwhile, in a large pan, heat the truffle oil for a few seconds. Add the mushrooms and season with salt and pepper. Cover and cook over a medium heat for about 5 minutes, stirring occasionally, until softened. Uncover and cook for a further 3 minutes, stirring, until lightly browned. Add the shallot and garlic and cook for a couple of minutes until softened. Stir in the parsley and sage, then season with salt and pepper.

Spoon the mushrooms over the cheese to serve.

Roasted Peach Camembert

4 large peaches, stoned and sliced

2½ tbsp balsamic vinegar, plus extra for drizzling

1 tbsp honey

2 tbsp olive oil

1 small garlic clove, finely chopped

1 x 250g (9oz) wheel of Camembert

(illustrated opposite, top left)

Preheat the oven to 200°C (400°F/Gas Mark 6).

Place the peaches on a baking sheet. In a small bowl, combine the balsamic vinegar, honey, oil and garlic. Pour this mix over the peaches and bake for 20 minutes.

Place the Camembert on a plate. Mound the peaches on top, and drizzle with a little extra vinegar. Enjoy with crackers or crusty bread.

Fig, Walnut and Honey Camembert

1 x 250g (9oz) wheel of Camembert

sprig of fresh thyme, leaves stripped

handful of broken walnuts

2 tsp honey

2 fresh figs, sliced into rounds

(illustrated opposite, top right)

Place the Camembert on a plate.

Scatter the cheese with the thyme and walnuts, add the fig slices and drizzle a little honey over.

Crème Brûlée Camembert

1 x 250g (9oz) wheel of Camembert in a box

60g (2oz) brown sugar

(illustrated opposite, bottom left)

Remove the Camembert from the box and unwrap it, then put the cheese back in the bottom half of the box, leaving the lid off. Using a small, sharp knife, cut a 'lid' out of the top of the cheese, making sure you don't cut all the way through to the bottom. Remove the 'lid', leaving the silky interior exposed.

Sprinkle the sugar on top of the Camembert, then place under the grill (broiler) or use a kitchen blowtorch to heat the sugar until it goes brown and hard. Serve with biscotti for dipping.

Honey and Pistachio Baked Camembert

1 x 250g (9oz) wheel of Camembert, in a box

2 tbsp honey

2 tbsp unsalted shelled pistachios

freshly ground black pepper

(illustrated opposite, bottom right)

Preheat the oven to 200°C (400°F/Gas Mark 6). Remove the Camembert from the box and unwrap it, then put the cheese back in the bottom half of the box, leaving the lid off. Cut the Camembert across three times, then again the other way. Place it on a baking sheet and bake for 15 minutes, or until bubbling.

Place the cheese on a serving dish, drizzle with the honey and sprinkle the shelled pistachios on top. Grind over a little black pepper and serve with farmhouse bread.

Truffled Cheese

Truffled cheese is about as indulgent as it gets. I absolutely love any cheese with truffles inside – the flavour is exquisite and no other cheese can compete. So imagine if you were able to make your own at home… The success lies in the quality of the cheese and truffles: the truffles must be lovely and fresh and at the peak of the season. You can use a soft cheese you have made, or a shop-bought Brie, Camembert or Coulommiers. The truffling technique can be applied to any unpasteurized soft rich cheese.

1 soft cheese, about 250g (9oz)

50g (1¾oz) mascarpone (see page 60)

2 tsp whipping cream

1 fresh black truffle, about 30–40g (1–1½oz) (preserved can be used too)

freshly ground black pepper

1 Cut the soft cheese in half horizontally, using a sharp knife.

2 In a large bowl, mix the mascarpone with the whipping cream.

3

4

3 Using a small peeler or truffle shaver, lightly peel the truffle, then shave half the truffle into the bowl. Stir to combine.

4 Using a palette knife, spread the mascarpone, cream and truffle mixture over the bottom half of the cheese, then add a little pepper.

5 Shave the rest of the truffle over the mascarpone mixture.

5

6 Place the top half of the cheese over the bottom half to form the original shape.

7 Lightly press down on the cheese, then wrap in clingfilm (plastic wrap) and place in the refrigerator for at least 24 hours, to let the truffle infuse.

8 Remember to remove the cheese from the refrigerator at least 1–2 hours before serving.

6

7

Accompaniments for Cheese

What better to eat alongside a hunk of cheese than a tasty side, and it's not hard to make your own at home.

Easy Homemade Butter in a Jar

I didn't realize how easy it was to make butter at home until I gave it a go – and now I love it. It tastes so fresh and far superior to shop-bought butter. You don't need any special equipment, and there are so many flavours you can add and experiment with. I was recently bought a mini butter churn, which makes it even easier.

300ml (10fl oz/1¼ cups) double (heavy) cream
salt and freshly ground black pepper

MAKES ABOUT 250g (9 oz)

You will need: 2 jars with a lid – mason jars work well, mini butter churn (optional)

1 Fill your first jar half full with cream, then screw the lid on, making sure it is secured tightly.

2 Now all you need to do is shake your jar up and down until you see the cream thicken and begin to form a ball of butter. The timings will depend on how quick and strong you are when shaking, so give it some elbow grease. It may take some time but it's a great workout and is well worth the wait. If you have a butter churn you can use that.

3 Open the jar and drain the liquid into a second jar. This is buttermilk and can be used in other recipes.

4 Now knead your butter under cold water for a few minutes, making sure you get rid of all the excess buttermilk (this is the messy bit).

5 Add a pinch of salt and pepper if desired, and mould the butter into any shape you like. This will keep in the refrigerator for up to 2 weeks and can also be frozen.

3

4

5

Jellies, Jams and Chutneys

You don't need fancy equipment to make condiments – it's a simple pleasure that makes the most of seasonal fruits so that they can be enjoyed for months to come. Homemade jellies, jams and chutneys make a brilliant gift, or will sit happily in your cupboard for months, ready and waiting for a beautiful piece of cheese.

Quince Jelly

1.5kg (3lb 5oz) quinces, unpeeled

750g (1lb 10oz) granulated sugar

4 tbsp fresh lemon juice

MAKES 500g (1lb 1¾oz)

Wash the quinces in cold water, then chop roughly and place them into a large saucepan with enough water to cover them. Simmer over a medium heat for 30 minutes until they are lovely and soft.

Drain the cooked quinces into a sieve (fine-mesh strainer), then push them through the sieve (strainer) with a wooden spoon into a bowl. The mixture should resemble a purée. Discard any remaining solids. Add the lemon juice.

Transfer the sieved mixture back into a clean saucepan with the sugar and place over a low heat. Keep stirring every 5 minutes and slowly bring the mixture to the boil, then cook for about 30 minutes. You should see the mixture becoming thicker. Keep stirring until it comes together, then take it off the heat.

Pour the mixture into a ceramic or metal loaf dish lined with clingfim (plastic wrap). It will set pretty quickly and will keep in the refrigerator for up to 6 months.

Chilli Jam

This recipe makes quite a sweet chilli jam. If you like it a bit hotter, use a chilli with a bit more bite.

600g (1lb 5oz) red chillies, deseeded and roughly chopped (wear gloves!)

450g (1lb) red (bell) peppers, deseeded and roughly chopped

1kg (2lb 3oz) granulated sugar

1 litre (1¾ pints/4 cups) white wine vinegar

2 tbsp salt

MAKES 2 JARS

Preheat the oven to its lowest setting. Place your sterilized jars in the oven to keep warm, so the glass doesn't break when filled with hot jam.

Meanwhile, place the chillies and red (bell) peppers into a food processor and pulse until smooth. Set aside.

Put the sugar and vinegar in a large saucepan and simmer over a low heat for 30 minutes until the sugar has totally dissolved. The consistency should be smooth, similar to a syrup. Add the chillies, peppers and salt and simmer for another 45 minutes.

Leave the jam to cool slightly – it should hold together well. Pour into the jars and leave to cool for a few hours before sealing. Then enjoy.

Fig Chutney

600g (1lb 5oz) fresh figs, chopped into small cubes

2 large apples, peeled, cored and chopped into small cubes

1 onion, chopped into small cubes

300g (10½oz) soft dark brown sugar

240ml (8½ fl oz/1 cup) apple cider vinegar

1 tsp salt

MAKES 2 JARS

Warm your jars as for the Chilli Jam. Meanwhile, place all the ingredients in a large saucepan over a low heat and simmer for 1 hour, stirring every 10 minutes, until the mixture is the consistency of jam.

Remove from the heat and leave to cool slightly. Pour into the jars and leave to cool for a few hours before sealing.

Cheese Pairings

When it comes to pairing cheese and any alcohol, there are a number of considerations, such as texture, acidity, fat and tannin. But the options are endless, and it really comes down to what you enjoy.

Cheese and Wine

Cheese and wine are two of life's great pleasures, so what is better than enjoying them together? And I have had a lot of fun over the years finding the perfect match!

A few tips I always use when pairing . . .
- Remember the following: what grows together, goes together. If a goat's cheese is the pride of the Loire Valley in France, try pairing it with wines from the Loire Valley.
- Pair wines with cheeses of equal intensity. There is no point in having a wine that will overpower the taste of the cheese – you want them to marry well. A good rule of thumb is that wines of over 14 per cent alcohol have a more intense flavour and will taste better with a stronger-tasting cheese. Wines under 12 per cent alcohol are less intense and match with a milder-tasting cheese.
- If you are a little overwhelmed and unsure which cheese to pair with which wine, a safe bet is to pair a red wine with a firm, nutty cheese. The cheese will have enough fat to counterbalance the tannin in the red wine.

FRESH CHEESE Feta, goat's cheese, mozzarella, ricotta and burrata pair very well with crisp, dry white wines – such as a young Chardonnay, Sauvignon blanc, Pinot gris, Chablis, Sancerre, Pinot noir, Gamay – and dry rosé wines, as well as sparkling wines. Just avoid big, tannic red wines as they will overpower the cheese.

My favourite pairing: Sainte Maure and Sauvignon blanc

SOFT CHEESE Soft cheeses such as Brie, Camembert, Neufchâtel, Baron Bigod and Tunworth are rich, buttery cheeses, which pair well with rich white wines or low-tannin fruity red wines. Champagne is fantastic with soft cheeses because the effervescence cuts through the richness of the cheese. Try pairing with good Champagne, Chardonnay, Sancerre, Chablis, Beaujolais, Côtes du Rhône and sparkling wines.

My favourite pairing: Tunworth English Camembert and Perrier-Jouët Champagne

SEMI-HARD CHEESE Semi-hard cheeses such as Comté, Gruyère, creamy Cheddar, young Gouda and fontina are well balanced with a firmer texture and stronger flavour. They go well with medium-bodied whites and fruity reds. Pair them with Chardonnay, white and red Burgundy, Pinot gris, Rioja, Pinot noir, Zinfandel, rosé, sherry and young port.

My favourite pairing: Westcombe Cheddar and white Bordeaux

HARD CHEESE Hard cheeses such as Parmigiano Reggiano, aged Gouda, cloth-bound Cheddar, manchego, Beaufort, Cantal, Emmental and pecorino are strong-flavoured and beautifully mature, so they match well with full-bodied whites and tannic reds, mirroring the intensity of the wine. Pair them with aged white Burgundy, Bordeaux, Cabernet Sauvignon, Shiraz, Merlot, vintage port, Muscat and sherry.

My favourite pairing: Pecorino sardo and Chianti

BLUE CHEESE Blue cheeses such as Stilton, Gorgonzola, fourme d'ambert, bleu d'Auvergne, Cabrales and Roquefort pair well with wines that are a little bit sweeter but still have a bite. This complements the saltiness of the cheese and balances the taste. Try Riesling, Vin santo, white Burgundy, Sauternes, Pinot noir, Shiraz, sparkling reds, Muscat and port.

My favourite pairing: Stilton and tawny port

'STINKY' CHEESE Washed-rind cheeses such as Taleggio, Epoisses, Pont L'Évêque, reblochon, Munster and vacherin mont d'or are strong and stinky, so try to pair them with wines that complement the cheese instead of trying to match the very strong flavours. These pair nicely with rich, fragrant wines, sweeter wines and full-bodied reds, such as Riesling, white Burgundy, Sauternes, Pinot gris, Pinot noir, Shiraz, sparkling reds, Muscat and port.

My favourite pairing: Taleggio and Merlot

complements the sweet and creamy taste of the cheese.
- IPA (India pale ale) goes well with a strong mature farmhouse Cheddar; the sharpness of the Cheddar pairs well with the hoppiness of the IPA.
- Pilsner pale lager is lovely with fresh cheese, such as goat's cheese and burrata. Pilsner is a light beer and goes well with the subtle flavours of the fresh cheese.
- Barley wine goes really well with stinky washed-rind cheeses, which are punchy and strong, as the barley wine is equally strong.
- Pair imperial stout with a strong spicy blue cheese, as they go really well with the roast flavours of stout.
- I like German lager with Alpine-style cheeses like Gruyère. The nutty flavour of the cheese complements the nutty, caramel flavours of the beer.
- Golden ale goes well with Parmesan, as the dryness of the beer accentuates the dry and sharply intense notes of aged Parmesan.

Cheese and Beer

There are no real rules for pairing cheese and beer – it is simply down to personal preference. Here are a few tips to help inspire and develop your own pairings that work for your personal taste.

- When buying beer, look for notes on the label that complement the flavour and texture notes of the cheese.
- When pairing cider (hard cider) and cheese, match the intensity of the cider with the intensity of the cheese. Cider is great with a creamy blue cheese that has a bit of a tangy and nutty bite; taking a sip of cider will help bring all of those big, bold flavours together.
- Belgian beers pair well with Gruyère, Emmental or Comté. Belgian beers have a yeasty flavour, which complements the nutty cheese.
- Sweet stout goes well with creamy blue cheese. The sweetness of the stout

Cheese and Whisky

Whisky as a food pairing is becoming more popular. Below are a few styles of whisky and some ideas of which cheeses to pair with them.

- A medium-bodied whisky goes really nicely with crottin de Chavignol, the most well-known type of goat's cheese. It has a nutty creaminess that pairs well with the whisky.
- A Scotch whisky goes really nicely with a salty, strong Comté cheese. The honey and vanilla taste of the Scotch marries beautifully with the Comté.
- Cashel blue is a rich, creamy milk cheese with tangy, sharp flavours that would overpower a lot of whisky, but a good 'Sherry Bomb' whisky can stand up against the strength of any quality blue cheese.

Cheese and Spirits

Although it may seem unusual, vodka is fantastic as a cheese pairing, and just like wine or beer, can enhance the flavour of cheese, too. I pair vodka with tangy, full-flavoured goat's cheese, and also with strong, crumbly cheeses such as manchego.

Gin is another great pairing. The gin has a light, dry taste that is beautifully fresh. When paired with a triple cream cheese, the cheese really brings out the delicious citrus and botanical flavours.

Seasonal Cheese Boards

Fruit, vegetables, meat and fish taste best when in season, and cheese is no different. Just as fruit and vegetables come in and out of season, the grasses and wildflowers eaten by cows, sheep and goats do the same. The milk produced by the animals reflects this changing diet, giving cheese different flavours and textures as the year progresses.

I love to create cheese boards that display the best of what each season has to offer. It also gives me an excuse to have a cheese party each time the seasons change, and get all my friends and family over to sample the best cheeses that each season has to offer.

On the following pages are my favourite cheese boards that represent the changing seasons.

Spring Cheese Board

When spring comes, temperatures warm up and cows return to the fields for grass and clover. The resulting milk sees fat and protein content drop, and cheeses tend to be brighter and lighter-bodied, with mellow flavours.

(Left to right) Beenleigh blue, Innes Bosworth Ash Log, Cornish Yarg and Brie de Meaux. With blackcurrant and bayleaf jam and rye crackers.

Summer Cheese Board

In summer, grasses and wildflowers flourish, so grazing animals have a rich and varied diet. This is one of my favourite months for cheese, because the summer milk has distinct floral notes, as well as complexity.

(Left to right) Cabrales, Neufchâtel, Cabri, Moliterno black truffle pecorino. With pears, honey and fresh bread.

Autumn Cheese Board

I love the colours of this cheese board: it just screams autumn.
As flowers and foliage die off, the milk becomes more
grassy, and with colder weather comes
a jump in butterfat and protein.

(Left to right) Mimolette, Valençay goat's cheese, Epoisses, Shropshire blue. With quince jelly, cheese biscuits and physalis.

Winter Cheese Board

Christmas is when a lot of us enjoy a good cheese board, and this is what I love to serve over the festive period. Over the winter, dairy cattle in temperate climates come in from the fields and eat grass that's been stored for the winter. Winter cheeses are often the creamiest with mild flavour profiles and grassy notes.

(Left to right) Tunworth English Camembert, Colston Bassett Stilton, Berkswell sheep's cheese, Etoile de Gâtine goat's cheese, Godminster oak-smoked Cheddar. With Bath Oliver crackers and fig and walnut cake.

Storing Cheese

In the cheese shop one of the most commonly asked questions is: 'How do you store cheese at home?'

For cheese, the 'good old days' were when we didn't have central heating, double glazing (double-paned windows) or fridges (refrigerators). Before the 1960s, many homes would have a pantry for storing food, which was usually located in the north-east corner of the house and remained cool throughout the year, at about 8–10°C (46–50°F). This created the perfect temperature and conditions for storing cheese.

Unfortunately, most of us now have centrally heated homes and larder fridges (refrigerators), which usually run at temperatures about 5°C (40°F) and dehydrate the cheese unless it's tightly wrapped.

Most good cheese shops will wrap your cheese in a breathable wax paper. If your cheese has not come in wax paper, the next best thing would be to wrap it in greaseproof (wax) paper and then wrap tightly in foil and pop it in the refrigerator. This will keep the cheese moist – while still allowing it to breathe – and safe from any flavour taint it may pick up from other foods stored nearby.

Clingfilm (plastic wrap) is a big no no for anything other than very short periods. All cheeses carry on maturing slowly in the store and in your refrigerator until they are consumed. When cheese wrapped in clingfilm (plastic wrap) matures, or if there is a rise in temperature, moisture will be drawn out of the cheese and trapped, causing the cheese to sweat. This can affect the flavour. Let the cheese breathe.

TEMPERATURE
The temperature at which cheese is kept really does depend on the individual cheese – for example, fresh and soft cheeses should be kept at a lower temperature in the main compartment of the refrigerator. Blue cheeses should also be kept in the refrigerator, but at the bottom in the salad crisper compartment. Harder cheeses are really best kept in a cool larder (pantry) if possible.

I would recommend taking all cheese out of the refrigerator 1½ to 2 hours before serving. I like to see the Brie running off the plate in front of me.

Similar to milk, cheese will taste a little high and sour when it is no longer edible.

BLUE CHEESE
If you have bought blue cheese, this too is better stored in greaseproof (wax) paper and foil as it keeps the cheese moist and allows the ripening process to continue unhindered.

If you keep blue cheese for longer than the use-by date, you may find the cut surface starts to bloom with a blue mould coat – don't worry, this is completely normal and the whole cheese remains edible. The cheese is just trying to form its own rind.

CHEESE TRUCKLES AND WHOLE CLOTH-WRAPPED CHEESES
A truckle or wheel of cheese is a living thing, maturing and developing over time – just like a fine bottle of wine. These are best kept in a larder (pantry) or other cool place. It's even better if you are lucky enough to have a cheese storage chest, as this is a fantastic way to keep cheese maturing until ready to serve.

Making the Most of your Cheese

Over one-third of all produce never reaches our plates. This is equivalent to 1.3 billion tonnes (metric tons) of food worldwide every year. If we reduced this by a quarter, there would be enough to feed everybody on the planet.

In wealthy countries, high levels of food waste are caused by food being discarded by consumers who have bought too much, or by retailers because the products don't meet aesthetic requirements.

In the cheese shop I encourage our customers to waste less. Cheese is one of the foods most commonly thrown away, but below are a few tips on making the most of your cheese.

MOULDY CHEESE
While soft cheeses and curds shouldn't be eaten if they go mouldy, hard cheeses are fine. Just cut off the mould and dig in, as the cheese is still edible.

PARMESAN RINDS
Don't throw them away! Add them to soups, stews or risottos, and as they cook down they add the most delicious flavour.

FREEZING
Most cheeses can be frozen. Grate hard cheese and freeze it in sandwich bags, ready to sprinkle straight onto pasta or pizza before cooking.

PESTO
Grate any hard cheese and blitz it with nuts, olive oil and basil to make a delicious pesto sauce that can be kept for up to a week.

NO-WASTE CHEESE SCONES
Use 200g (7oz) of any cheese you have left over, including blue, and follow my recipe for Cheese and Garlic Scones on page 148. You'll have a big mound of cheesiness without wasting a thing.

BUY SMALL
My best bit of advice is, whenever possible, to buy your cheese in small quantities. This way you can Buy. Eat. Repeat.

Sourcing Ingredients and Equipment

Additives and cultures

Calcium chloride

Calcium chloride is needed when the milk used for cheesemaking has been pasteurized or homogenized. During processing, the chemical structure of milk is changed, sometimes drastically. Those changes include a slight decrease in calcium levels within the milk. Calcium is necessary for proper curd formation. By adding calcium chloride to the milk before adding the coagulant, calcium levels are restored. Calcium chloride is commonly used in making some goat cheeses, which can have a less firm curd due to the natural homogenization of goat's milk.

Fresh charcoal, for coating

Ash, sometimes called activated charcoal, is a food-grade charcoal used on some soft cheeses to neutralize the surface of the cheese, creating a friendly environment for the growth of Penicillium candidum. Your cheese will usually develop a blue-grey, mottled rind with a nutty texture and a strong creamy flavour. I often use it with goat's cheese.

Lipase powder

Lipase is an enzyme used in cheesemaking to create a stronger or sharper flavour. It also helps to develop a distinctive aroma. Lipase powder is used often in Italian cheeses such as Parmesan, provolone and fontina.

Mesophilic culture

Mesophilic direct-set culture are used for soft-ripened and fresh cheeses including Brie, Camembert, havarti, Gouda, Edam, feta, blue and chèvre.

Thermo B culture

Thermophile Type B starter culture can be used to make a variety of Italian-style cheeses, including mozzarella, romano, provolone and grana.

Penicillium candidum

Penicillium candidum – white mould powder – is used to ripen and flavour Brie, Camembert, Coulommiers and a variety of other French goat's cheeses. It produces a nice white bloom on the surface of your cheese.

Penicillium roqueforti is a type of

mould spore used for making blue cheese. The spores start growing from the outside in, creating a white crust on the cheese before infusing the interior and producing a soft, creamy consistency with a distinctive aroma. It provides the characteristic appearance of the cheese, contributing to fast growth rate, the strong blue-cheese flavour, blue-green colour and creamy consistency.

Propionic shermanii

Propionic Shermanii produces the characteristic aroma and flavour associated with Swiss, Gruyère and Emmental-style cheese.

UK suppliers

www.cheesemakingshop.co.uk
www.amazon.co.uk
www.gnltd.co.uk
www.lakeland.co.uk

Worldwide

www.cheesemaking.com
www.thecheesemaker.com
www.amazon.com

Cheesemaking equipment

For strainers, filters, testers, mats, thermometers, curd knives, cheese irons (for testing aged cheese), pH and acidity testers, cheese cloths/muslin, cheese-wrapping paper, sanitizers, gloves, and various other useful pieces of equipment, such as cheese presses and moulds and the Kilner butter churner.

UK suppliers

www.amazon.co.uk
www.cheesemakingshop.co.uk
www.gnltd.co.uk
www.cheesemaking.co.uk
www.lakeland.co.uk

Worldwide

www.amazon.com
www.cheesemaking.com
www.thecheesemaker.com

Waxes

Black, red and natural waxes.

UK suppliers

www.cheesemakingshop.co.uk

Worldwide

www.cheesemaking.com
www.thecheesemaker.com

Serving cheese

Assorted knives for hard and soft cheeses, graters, cutting wires, boards, cheese curlers and slicers and cheese preservers for storing your cheese in optimum condition. Cheese bakers, raclette makers and fondue pots. Specialist ingredients such as black truffle.

UK suppliers

www.cheesemaking.co.uk
www.lakeland.co.uk

Worldwide

www.boska.com

Cheeses from Round the World: Morgan's Selection

Australia

Ashgrove Cheese: Cheddar
Berrys Creek Gourmet Cheese: Riverine Blue
Drysdale Cheeses: Bellarine Blu
King Island Dairy: Roaring Forties Blue
Nimbin Valley Dairy: Orange Billy
Prom Country Cheese: Prom Picnic
Pyengana Dairy: Clothbound Cheddar
Woodside Cheese Wrights: Blackwood Orana

Austria

Almenland Stollenkäse: Capellaro
Biosennerei Kolsass: Bio Korbkäse mit Pfeffer
Concept Fresh: Ein gutes Stück Heimat Bio-Ziegenfrischkäse Natur
Furore: Bregenzerwälder Ursalzkäse
Gebrüder Woerle: S-Budget Frischkäse Kräuter
Obersteirische Molkerei: Rahmsteirer
Premiumkaeserei Pranz: Schaf royal
Rupp AG: Alma Vorarlberger Bergkäse (matured at least 10 months)

Vorarlberg Milch: Ländle Rahmkäse
Weizer Schafbauern: S' Würzige Schaf

Belgium

ID Fresh: Frontieren Brokkel
Kaasboerderij 't Groendal: Old Groendal
L'Art du Fromage: Oudlander
Le Larry: hard goat's milk farmers' cheese

Bosnia and Herzegovina

Orman Farmersko Blago: Livanjski sir Reserve – matured at least 12 months

Canada

Fromagerie Fuoco: Fuoco
Fromagerie la Station: Alfred le Fermier 24 mois
Saputo Dairy Products: Chèvre des Neiges Miel; Snowgoat Honey
Société Coopérative Agricole de l'Isleaux-Grues: Le Riopelle de l'Isle

Croatia

Agrolaguna: Istarski miješ ani sir u orahovom liš' u – Špin
Paška Sirana: Pramenko
Sirana Gligora: Liburjan

Cyprus

A.P. Polycarpou and Sons Farm: Halloumi
Charalambos Christis: Biological Halloumi; Kefalotyri
Pittas Dairy Industries: Cow, goat and sheep's milk Halloumi

Denmark

Dutch Deli :Biokaas Kinderdijk organic goat cheese – extra matured
Grand fromage: Lihmskov Extra
Knuthenlund: Fårebrie
Sønderhaven Gårdmejeri: Comendante 45+

France

Abbaye Notre-Dame de Belloc: Abbaye de Belloc
Arnaud Family: Gour Noir
Beillevaire: Camembert de Normandie
Berthaut: Epoisses; Soumaintrain
Burgat Family Farm: Tomme
Chevrechard: Clochette
Fromagerie de Terre Dieu: Lavort; Patrick Beaumont Fumaison
Fromagerie du Petit Morin: Explorateur
Fromagerie Ganot: Brie
Fromagerie Gaugry: L'Ami du Chambertin
Fromagerie E. Graindorge: Livarot
Fromagerie Guilloteau: Campagnier
Fromagerie Lincet: Délice de Bourgogne
Fromagerie Rouzaire: Brillat-Savarin
Isigny Sainte-Mère: Brie
Jacquard: Valençay
La Ferme du Petit Mont: Raclette
Lactalis: P'tit Basque
Laiteries H. Triballat: La Brebette

Le Châtelain: Camembert
Maison Fischer: Grès des Vosges
Onetik: Ossau Iraty Grande Réserve
Papillon: Roquefort Papillon
Poitou-Chèvre: Delice des Deux-Sèvres
Savencia Fromage & Dairy: Saint Agur
SégalaFrom: Bouyguette
Sèvre et Belle: Bucherondin; Le Chevrot
Société Laitière de Laqueuille: 1924 Bleu

Germany
Heinrichsthaler: Bierkäse
Rohmilchkaeserei Backensholz: Deichkäse

Greece
Arvanitis: Feta Arvaniti
Karavitis Potis & Yioi M.: Graviera Manis E
Kourellas: Kourellas Says Organic Anevato

Ireland
Bandon Vale Cheese: Dunnes Stores Single
    Bath Selection Graders Choice Block
Inagh Farmhouse Cheese: St Tola Ash Log
Killeen Farmhouse Cheese: Killeen Goat
Old Irish Creamery Cheese: Natural Oak
    Smoked Cheddar
Traditional Cheese Co: Dunnes Stores Delicate
    and Smooth Goat's Ricotta Cheese

Italy
L'Agricola: Blu di Capra
Azienda Agricola e Zootecnica Posticchia Sabelli:
    Caciocavallo
Carmelina Colantuono: Caciocavallo Podolico
Carozzi formaggi: Capriziola
Casa Madaio: Barilotto; Mozzarella Bufala
Caseificio Bertagni: Formaggio al Tartufo
Caseificio Busti: Il Pecorino Toscano DOP
    Semistagionato
Caseificio Il Fiorino: Riserva Del Fondatore
Caseificio Sepertino: Caciottina di capra
Castelli: Gorgonzola Piccante PDO
Central Formaggi: Moliterno al Tartufo; Pastore
    Central
Clarke Gemini International: Gran Vittoria Dolce
    Gorgonzola DOP
Consorzio Conva-Nazionale del Parmigiano
    Reggiano: Nazionale del Parmigiano Reggiano
    4 Madonne Caseificio dell'Emilia
Consorzio Gourm.it: Madama Reale –
    Caseificio Pier Luigi Rosso; Asiago Stagionato
    Dop – Cas. San Rocco Soc. Coop. Agricola
Cora Formaggi: Ciabot
De' Magi: Pinetta
Fausto Caserio (Italian food hunters): Marzolina
La Casearia Carpenedo: Blu '61
Paolo Farabegoli: Pecorino
Quattro Portoni: Blu di Bufala
Società Cooperativa Val d'Orcia: Pecorino Toscano
Vallet Pietro: Fontina

Netherlands
Beemster: Signature
Daily Dairy: VSOC White Label
De Graafstroom: De Graafstroom Oud 30+

Lindenhoff: Gouda
Remeker: Remeker Pracht
Uniekaas: 5-year-old Gouda
Uniekaas with De Producent: Melkbus 149 Truffle
Vandersterre Holland: Boer'n Trots honey goat truffle

Norway
Aalan gård: Capra
Bo Jensen Dairy: Lille Aske
Gangstad Gårdsysteri: Edel Blå Large
Rueslåtten Ysteri: Rød Geit
Tine: Kvit Geitost Lagra
Tingvollost: Edel Frue

Portugal
Indulac Martin S&Rebello: Goat's Milk Cheese
    Reserve Edition
Sonae Mc: Queijo de Azeitão DOP Continente
    Seleção

Slovakia
Gorski: Gorski zreli sir

Serbia
Leonteus: Hard goat's milk cheese 6 months old

South Africa
Belnori Boutique Cheesery: Kilembe
    Dalewood Fromage Dalewood Huguenot
Klein River Cheese: Klein River Matured Gruberg

Spain
Agricola La Merced: Chisquero Semicurado
Agroalimentaria Valle de los Molinos: Pago Valle
    de los Molinos matured with Rosemary
Agropecuaria Navalnoshaces: Pozueleño Curado
    En Manteca; Navaloshaces Semicurado
Alcalaten: Queso Tierno El Becerril
Aldanondo Corporacion Alimentaria: Urepel Bleu
Alimentos de Miraflores: Peñagorda queso
    curado de cabra
Asoc. Queserias Artesanales Delanzarote (AQUAI):
    Semicurado Tinache
Arteserena: El Eprimijo
Balcobo Agropecuaria: 1605 Curado
Biogranja Montesdeoca: Queso Curado Cabra
    Oregano
Cabildo De Gran Canaria: La Gloria Curado
    De Cabra
Cañarejal: Cañarejal Cremoso
Capsa Food: Queso Cabrales Cueva del Molin
Casa Mateu: Tou de Casa Mateu
Central Quesera Montesinos: Cana de Cabra
Chacon e Hijo: Lomo Gallego, Semi-Hard With
    Pimenton
Coinga: Queso Curado Sa Naveta Dop
    Mahonmenorca
Como Cabras, S. Coop. Galega: Touza Vella
Cortijo el Aserradero: Cortijo el Aserradero
De La Huz Grimaldos Industrias Lácteas: De La
    Huz Sheep and Goat Cheese Semi-Aged
Dehesa de Los: Llanos Manchego DOP Gran
    Reserva
Don Merendon: Inanna
El Buen Pastor de Oropesa: Queso de Oveja

curado en Bodega
Enrique: Malvarosa
Esperanza del Castillo: Manchego Cured
Fermin Tordesillas Casals: Castell-Llebre
Finca De Uga: Vulcano
Formatge Baridà: Formatge Baridà
Formatgeria La Cleda: Tacat de Tòfona
Formatges Artesans De Ponent: Formatge
    Curat De Cabra
Formatges Mas El Garet: Garrotxa ecològic
Francisco Moran e Hijos: Queso Francisco
    Sudao
Fundació Ampans: Formatge blau de cabra
Gestion Agro Ganadera: La Antigua con
    Pimienta Negra
Granja Cantagrullas: Braojos Cantagrullas
Grupo Ganaderos De Fuerteventura: Maxorata
    semicurado pimentón
Herederos de Felix Sanz: Queso Semicurado
    Campoveja
Hermanos Sadornil Castrillo: Mantecoso de
    Oveja
Hijos De Salvador Rodriguez: Sheep's Milk
    Cheese Manche GO DOP 3 Months
Ilbesa: Queso Mezcla Madurado Luyan
Ilujor Orcajo Garcia: Queso Curado Artesano
Joseba Insausti Mujika: Otatza
La Cabaña: Rosemary Manchego
Lácteas Garcia Baquero: Garcia Baquero
    Cinco Lanzas
Lácteos el pastor del valle: Queso curado de
    cabra al romero
Lácteos Lanjaron: Queso de Cabra Añejo
    Curado en Aceite de Oliva Virgen Extra
Lácteos Martinez: Los Cameros PDO Queso
    Camerano
Lácteos Segarra: Cured Goat Cheese Caprillice
Pasamontes: Manchego
Quesera Campo Rus: Campo Rus al Azafran
Queseria 1605: Manchego
Queseria Doña Fancisca: Queso De Cabra
    Sudao
Queseria El Roano: Queso Curado de Leche
    Cruda El Roano
Queseria Finca Pascualete: Miniretorta
Queseria Los Casareños: Torta Del Casar Dop
    Flor De La Dehesa
Quesos Corcuera: Campo de Montalbán
Quesos de Almazora: Queso Semicurado
    De Oveja
Quesos Del Casar: Torta Del Casar DOP Gran
    Casar; Viejo Maestro
Quesos El Bosqueño: El Bosqueño Cabra
    Payoya En Manteca Ibérica
Quesos Elvira Garcia: Canto Viejo
Quesos Marsan: Marsan Semicurado; Campo
    Oro Curado
Quesos Navalmoral: Manchego PDO
    Navalmoral Viejo
Quesos Quevedo: Queso de Oveja Semicurado
Quesos Revilla: Queso Viejo de Oveja Leche
    Cruda Platería
Quesos Vega Sotuelamos: Pasteurized Sheep
    Cheese With Truffle
Quorum Internacional: Manchego PDO Gran

Valle de Montecelo, 12 months
Rafael Baez: Monte Enebro
S.A.T. Queso Flor Valsequillo: Semi ahumado
    queso flor valsequillo
Serones Artesano: Serones Artesano
Son Vives: Queso Son Vives Semicurado
Subaida: Semicurado Subaida
Tierra de Barros: Tortita de Barros
Villa Villera: Queso Curado mezcla Vaca Oveja

Sweden
Jürss Mejeri: Granbarksost

Switzerland
Alois Pfister: Appenzeller
Alpages of Switzerland: La Case 6299 Etivaz
    Organic AOP
Fromagerie Le Cret: Gruyère (1655 Le Cret)
Herr Glauser: Belper Knolle
Jumi: Blue Brain
Kaeseri Steinen: Hanfmutschli
Lustenberger & Dürst: Emmentaler AOP Antique
    Langrüti 1862; St Jost LeSuperbe; Sbrinz AOP
    LeSuperbe
Sepp Barmettler: Stanser Fladä
Val d'Arve SA Groupe Laiteries Rèunies Genève:
    Blanches
Von Mühlenen: Vacherin Fribourgeois Classic;
    Vacherin Fribourgeois Rustic
Walo von Mühlenen: mature

Turkey
AK GIDA: çim Süzme Beyaz Peynir

United Kingdom
Abergavenny Fine Foods: Dunnes Stores Honey &
    Ginger Goats Cheese
Alsop & Walker: Mayfield
Appleby Creamery: Eden Valley Brie; Nanny Mcbrie
Appleby's: Appleby's Cheshire
Ashley Chase Estate: Cave-aged cheddar
Bath Soft Cheese Co.: Bath Soft Cheese
Barbers Farmhouse Cheesemakers: Vintage
    Farmhouse Cheddar (PDO)
Blackwoods Cheese Co.: Graceburn
Brinkworth Dairy: Royal Bassett Blue
Burt's Cheese: Burt's Blue
Butlers Farmhouse Cheeses: Blacksticks Blue
Caerfai Farm: Caerfai Cheddar
Cashel Farmhouse Cheesemakers/J&L Grubb
    Ltd: Cashel Blue
Caws Cenarth Cheese: Golden Cenarth
Cerney Cheese: Cerney Ash Pyramid
Charles Martell & Son Ltd: Stinking Bishop
Colston Bassett Dairy: Shropshire Blue
Cornish Cheese Co.: Cornish Blue; Cornish Gouda
Cote Hill Cheese: Cote Hill Blue
Cow Close Farm: Stanage Millstone
Cropwell Bishop Creamery: Blue Stilton
Crudges Cheese: Sarsden
Curds and Croust: The Truffler; Boy Laity
Curworthy Cheese: Devon Oke
Doddington Dairy: Admiral Collingwood
Dunlop Dairy: Aiket; Clerkland Crowdie
Durrus Farmhouse Cheese: Durrus Cheese

Errington Cheese: Lanark Blue; Dunsyre Blue
Felthams Farm Cheeses: Renegade Monk
Fen Farm Dairy: Baron Bigod
Fielding Cottage: Wensum White
First Milk Cheese Company: Extra Mature Cheddar
Fowlers of Earlswood: Original Sage Derby
F. W. Read & Sons Ltd/Lincolnshire Poacher
  Cheese: Lincolnshire Poacher
Godfrey C. Williams and Son: Wensleydale and
  Cranberry
Godminster: Cheddar
Golden Cross Cheese Co. Ltd: Golden Cross
  Log; Flower Marie
Gringa Dairy: Queso Oaxaca
Hampshire Cheeses: Tunworth
Highland Fine Cheeses: Fearn Abbey
High Weald Dairy Ltd: Duddleswell
Innes Cheese: Bosworth Ash Log
Isle of Wight Cheese Co.: Isle of Wight Blue
J. A. & E. Montgomery Ltd: Montgomery Mature
  Cheddar
J.J. Sandham: Lancashire
Kappacasein: Bermondsey Hard Pressed
Keen's Cheddar: Keen's Unpasteurised
  Traditional Cheddar
Kupros Dairy: Anglum
Leicestershire Handmade Cheese Co.:
  Battlefield Blue; Sparkenhoe
Longley Farm: Cottage Cheese
Lyburn Farmhouse Cheesemakers: Francis
Lye Cross Farm: Mature Cheddar
Lynher Dairies Cheese Company: Yarg; Cornish Kern
Mike's Fancy Cheese: Young Buck
Monkland Cheese Dairy: Blue Monk
Neal's Yard Creamery: Dorstone
Nettlebed Creamery: St Bartholomew

Northumberland Cheese Company: Brinkburn;
  Nettle
Norton and Yarrow Cheese: Sinodun Hill
Olianas: Yorkshire Pecorino
Quicke's: Mature Clothbound Cheddar
Ram Hall Farm: Berkswell
Ribblesdale Cheese: Original Goat; Superior Goat
River Amble Creamery: 50 Jack
Sharpham Dairy: Sharpham Rustic
Shepherds Purse: Bluemin White; Mrs Bell's Blue
Smarts Traditional Gloucester Cheese: Double
  Gloucester
Somerset Cheese Company: Fosse Way Fleece
South Caernarfon Creameries: Caerphilly
St Andrews Farmhouse Cheese Company: Anster
St Helen's Farm: Goat's Cheese Deli Wheel
Stichelton Dairy Ltd: Stichelton
Swaledale Cheese Company: Swaledale Goats
  Milk Cheese
Teesdale Cheesemakers: Teesdale Goat
Tenacres Cheese: Hebden Goat
Thornby Moor Dairy: Crofton; Blue Whinnow
Ticklemore Cheese: Beenleigh Blue
Traditional Cheese Dairy: Lord of the Hundreds
Trethowan's Dairy: Gorwydd Caerphilly
Treveador Farm Dairy: Helford Blue
Two Hoots Cheese: Barkham Blue
Village Maid Cheese: Spenwood; Waterloo
Wensleydale Creamery: Yorkshire Wensleydale;
  Kit Calvert Old-style Wensleydale
West Highland Dairy: Highland Blue
Westcombe Dairy: Ducketts Caerphilly;
  Westcombe Cheddar
White Lake Cheese: Farleigh Wallop
White Wood Dairy: St Jude; St Cera
Yorkshire Dama Cheese: Matured yogurt balls

United States
Andante Dairy: Acapella
Artisan Cheese Exchange: Deer Creek; The Robin
Avalanche Cheese Company: Midnight Blue
BelGioioso: American Grana
Baetje Farms: Miette
Beehive Cheese Company: Promontory; Tea Hive
Bellwether Farms: Blackstone
Bleating Heart Cheese: Fat Bottom Girl
Boston Post Dairy: Smoking Goud
Capriole Goat Cheeses: Mont St Francis; Flora
Carr Valley Cheese Company: Ba Ba Blue;
  Shepherds Blend
Cellars at Jasper Hill: Little Hosmer
Central Coast Creamery: Dream Weaver
Chapel Hill Creamery: Hickory Grove
Charleston Artisan Cheesehouse: Battery Park
Cowgirl Creamery: Clabbered Cottage Cheese
Crave Brothers Farmstead Classics: Petit Frère
  with Truffles
Cypress Grove: Lamb Chopper; Fromage
  Blanc; Chevre Log; Midnight Moon
Deer Creek: Cheddar
Farm Fromage: Angela's Pillow
Firefly Farms: Merry Goat Round Spruce Reserve
Fruition Farms: Cacio Pecora
Goat Lady Dairy: Providence
Grafton Village: Barn Dance
Great Lakes Cheese: Adams Reserve Cheddar
Haystack Mountain Goat Dairy: Gold Hill
Jacobs and Brichford: Ameribella
Jasper Hill Farm: Alpha Tolman
Kennebec Cheesery: Chamoose
LaClare Family Creamery: Evalon
Landmark Creamery: Petit Nuage
Laura Chenel's Chevre: Ash-rinded Buchette

Leelanau Cheese Company: Aged Raclette
MouCo Cheese Company: Ashley
Nettle Meadow Farm and Artisan Cheese:
  Early Snow
Nicasio Valley Cheese Company: Nicasio Reserve
Old Chatham Sheepherding Company:
  Gatekeeper; Kinderhook Creek; Kinderhook
  Creek Mini
Parish Hill Creamery: Suffolk Punch
Point Reyes Farmstead Cheese Company: Bay Blue
Prairie Fruits Farm and Creamery: Black Sheep
Rogue Creamery: Rogue River Blue
Roth: Grand Cru Surchoix
Saputo Cheese: Kiss My Ash
Sartori Cheese: Sartori Reserve Black Pepper
  Bella Vitano
Sequatchie Cove Creamery: Cumberland
Silvery Moon Creamery: Smoked Provolone
Spring Brook Farm Cheese: Tarentaise
Springside Cheese: Aged Cheddar
Sweet Grass Dairy: Asher Blue
Twig Farm: Twig Farm Goat Tomme
Uplands Cheese: Rush Creek Reserve;
  Pleasant Ridge Reserve
Valley Shepherd Creamery: Crema de Blue
Vermont Creamery: Cremont; Goat Cheese
Vermont Shepherd: Verano; Invierno
Von Trapp Farmstead: Mad River Blue
Willow Hill Farm: Summertomme

Index

accompaniments for cheese 202–5
acid 14, 20
Affineur Walo 165
aligot 169
animal rennet 14, 20
apples: grilled Brie with caramelized apple
  and honey 80
artichokes: baked mozzarella, artichoke and
spinach dip 50
asparagus: Cheddar and veggie frittata 144
autumn cheeseboard 214–15
avocados: paneer spring rolls 108

bacon
  tartiflette 82
  tortellini bake 166
bake, tortellini 166
basil: ricotta and basil pesto 40
beer, cheese and 208–9
beetroot (beet), mint, fennel and feta salad
  132
Bellelay 116
Bio Hombre 172
Blackwoods Cheese Company 34
blue cheese 174–87, 207, 218
  baked eggs with blue cheese 185

blue cheese tarte tatin 186
  homemade 178–83
bread
  Camembert with Calvados 194
  classic croque monsieur 162
  Comté, ham and onion Sunday brunch
  rolls 170
  grilled Brie with caramelized apple and
  honey 80
  Welsh rarebit 143
Brie 78
  Brie de Meaux Dongé 69
  grilled Brie with caramelized apple and
  honey 80
brunch rolls, Comté, ham and onion Sunday
  170
burrata 52–5
  burrata and lemon penne 59
  burrata and tomato salad 56
butter: easy homemade butter in a jar 202
butternut squash soup with Comté 171

Calvados, Camembert with 194
Camembert 191
  Camembert with Calvados 194
  the classic baked Camembert 192

crème brûlée Camembert 196
  fig, walnut and honey baked Camembert 196
  honey and pistachio Camembert 196
  mushroom, garlic and truffle Camembert 194
  Parma ham-wrapped Camembert 194
  roasted peach Camembert 196
Capriole 91
carrots: paneer spring rolls 108
Casa Madaio 59
Cheddar 138–41
  Cheddar and veggie frittata 144
  cheese and garlic scones 148
  mature clothbound Cheddar 142
  tortellini bake 166
  very naughty mac and cheese 146
  Welsh rarebit 143
cheese
  accompaniments 202–5
  blue cheese 174–87, 207
  cream and soft cheeses 66–83
  fresh cheese 26–65, 206
  goat's cheese 84–97
  hard cheese 134–73, 207
  making the most of 219
  pairings 206–9
  semi-hard cheese 98–133, 207

serving 18
  soft cheese 207
  'stinky' cheese 207
  storing 218
cheese straws 116
cheeseboards, seasonal 209–17
cheesecake, lemon and raspberry ricotta 42
cheesemaking 8–9
  basic steps 20–5
  history of 8
  seasons 11
cheesemonger tips 188–219
chillies
  chilli jam 205
  jalapeño and Parmesan crisps 172
chocolate: mascarpone chocolate pots with
  homemade honeycomb 64
chutney, fig 205
cloth-wrapped cheeses 218
coconut milk: paneer, potato and coconut
  curry 110
Colston Bassett Dairy 185
Comté 137
  butternut squash soup with Comté 171
  Comté, ham and onion Sunday brunch
  rolls 170

cornichons: easy raclette at home 118
Cornish Yarg 137
cottage cheese 74–7
Coup de Corne 87
courgettes (zucchini)
    courgette and feta fritters 130
    courgette and goat's cheese tart 94
    red Leicester, cherry tomato and courgette
    tarts 154
Cows Creamery 148
cow's milk 12
cream
    aligot 169
    cream cheese 70
    easy homemade butter in a jar 202
    mascarpone 60–3
    mascarpone chocolate pots with homemade
    honeycomb 64
cream cheese 70
    lemon and raspberry ricotta cheesecake 42
    salmon, cream cheese and dill pancakes 72
crème brûlée Camembert 196
crisps, jalapeño and Parmesan 172
croque monsieur, classic 162
Crottin de Chavignol 87
curd cheese 30
    curd cheese dip 34
curry, paneer, potato and coconut 110
Cypress Grove 96

Delice de Bourgogne 29
digestive biscuits: lemon and raspberry ricotta
    cheesecake 42
dill: salmon, cream cheese and dill pancakes 72
dipping sauce, peanut butter 108
dips
    baked mozzarella, artichoke and spinach dip 50
    curd cheese dip 34
    yoghurt dip 130

eggs
    baked eggs with blue cheese 185
    Cheddar and veggie frittata 144
    Comté, ham and onion Sunday brunch
    rolls 170
    Red Leicester, cherry tomato and courgette
    tarts 154
    Welsh rarebit 143
Emmental: cheese fondue 165
Epoisses 69
equipment 17–18

fennel: beetroot, mint, fennel and feta salad 132
feta 126–9
    beetroot, mint, fennel and feta salad 132
    courgette and feta fritters 130
figs
    fig chutney 205
    fig, walnut and honey baked Camembert
    196
filo pastry: goat's cheese and spinach filo
    swirls 96
fish: salmon, cream cheese and dill pancakes 72
flavouring cheese 190–7
fondue, cheese 165
fontina: tortellini bake 166
Formatges Camps, Spain 182
freezing cheese 219
frittata, Cheddar and veggie 144
fritters, courgette and feta 130
Fromagerie Ganot 80
Fromagerie Graindorge 191

garlic
    cheese and garlic scones 148
    mushroom, garlic and truffle Camembert 194
gnocchi: homemade gnocchi with ricotta and
    basil pesto 40
goat's cheese 84–97
    courgette and goat's cheese tart 94
    creamy goat's cheese 88–90
    crumbly goat's cheese 92
    goat's cheese and spinach filo swirls 96
goat's milk 14
    creamy goat's cheese 88–90
    crumbly goat's cheese 92
Gouda 156–9
    Gouda, Parmesan and spinach rolls 161
green beans: paneer stuffed peppers 107
Gruyère
    aligot 169
    cheese fondue 165
    classic croque monsieur 162

halloumi 120–3
    warm Puy lentil, cherry tomato and
    halloumi salad 124
ham
    baked eggs with blue cheese 185
    classic croque monsieur 162
    Comté, ham and onion Sunday brunch rolls 170
    Parma ham-wrapped Camembert 194
Hereford Hop 101
honey
    fig, walnut and honey baked Camembert 196
    grilled Brie with caramelized apple and
    honey 80
    honey and pistachio Camembert 196
honeycomb, homemade 64

ingredients 12–14

jalapeño and Parmesan crisps 172
jam, chilli 205
jelly, quince 204

Karditsel 91
Kostarelos Dairy 132

labneh 29
lemons
    burrata and lemon penne 59
    lemon and raspberry ricotta cheesecake 42
lentils: warm Puy lentil, cherry tomato and
    halloumi salad 124

mascarpone 60–3
    mascarpone chocolate pots with
    homemade honeycomb 64
Meadow Creek Dairy 82
microbial rennet 14, 20
milk 12–14, 20
mint: beetroot, mint, fennel and feta salad 132
Morbier 101
mouldy cheese 219
mozzarella 29, 44–9
    aligot 169
    baked mozzarella, artichoke and spinach dip 50
    burrata 52–5
mushroom, garlic and truffle Camembert 194
my dreamy baked vacherin 192

Neufchâtel 69

Old Amsterdam 158

olives: blue cheese tarte tatin 186
onions: Comté, ham and onion Sunday
    brunch rolls 170
Ossau-Iraty 137

Paccard, Joseph 118
pancakes, salmon, cream cheese and dill 72
paneer 102–5
    paneer, potato and coconut curry 110
    paneer spring rolls with peanut butter
    dipping sauce 108
    paneer stuffed peppers 107
Parma ham-wrapped Camembert 194
Parmesan 219
    Gouda, Parmesan and spinach rolls 161
    jalapeño and Parmesan crisps 172
parsley: curd cheese dip 34
pasta
    burrata and lemon penne 59
    tortellini bake 166
    very naughty mac and cheese 146
peaches: roasted peach Camembert 196
peanut butter dipping sauce 108
peas
    paneer, potato and coconut curry 110
    paneer stuffed peppers 107
peppers
    blue cheese tarte tatin 186
    paneer spring rolls 108
    paneer stuffed peppers 107
pesto 219
    ricotta and basil pesto 40
pine nuts: burrata and lemon penne 59
pistachios: honey and pistachio Camembert 196
potatoes
    aligot 169
    Cheddar and veggie frittata 144
    easy raclette at home 118
    homemade gnocchi with ricotta and basil
    pesto 40
    paneer, potato and coconut curry 110
    tartiflette 82
provolone: jalapeño and Parmesan crisps 172
puff pastry
    blue cheese tarte tatin 186
    cheese straws 116
    courgette and goat's cheese tart 94
    Gouda, Parmesan and spinach rolls 161

Quattro Portoni 42
Quicke's Farm 144
quince jelly 204

Raclette 101
    easy raclette at home 118
raspberries: lemon and raspberry ricotta
    cheesecake 42
reblochon: tartiflette 82
red Leicester 150–3
    red Leicester, cherry tomato and courgette
    tarts 154
    Welsh rarebit 143
rennet 14, 20
ricotta 36
    lemon and raspberry ricotta cheesecake 42
    ricotta and basil pesto 40
    very indulgent ricotta 38
rocket: burrata and lemon penne 59
rolls, Gouda, Parmesan and spinach 161
Roquefort Papillon 186
rosemary
    the classic baked Camembert 192

my dreamy baked vacherin 192

St Maure 87
salads
    beetroot, mint, fennel and feta salad 132
    burrata and tomato salad 56
    warm Puy lentil, cherry tomato and halloumi
    salad 124
salmon, cream cheese and dill pancakes 72
salt 14
scones
    cheese and garlic scones 148
seasons, cheese 11
shallots: curd cheese dip 34
sheep's milk 14
Shropshire blue 177
smoked salmon, cream cheese and dill
    pancakes 72
soup: butternut squash soup with Comté 171
Spanish Cabrales 177
spinach
    baked eggs with blue cheese 185
    baked mozzarella, artichoke and spinach dip 50
    goat's cheese and spinach filo swirls 96
    Gouda, Parmesan and spinach rolls 161
spirits, cheese and 209
spring cheeseboard 210–11
spring rolls: paneer spring rolls with peanut
    butter dipping sauce 108
squash: butternut squash soup with Comté 171
storing cheese 218
summer cheeseboard 212–13
swirls, goat's cheese and spinach filo 96
Swiss cheese 112–15
    cheese straws 116

tartiflette 82
tarts
    blue cheese tarte tatin 186
    courgette and goat's cheese tart 94
    red Leicester, cherry tomato and courgette
    tarts 154
tomatoes
    blue cheese tarte tatin 186
    burrata and tomato salad 56
    paneer stuffed peppers 107
    red Leicester, cherry tomato and courgette
    tarts 154
    warm Puy lentil, cherry tomato and halloumi
    salad 124
truckles 218
truffle oil: mushroom, garlic and truffle
    Camembert 194
truffled cheese 198–201

vacherin mont d'or, my dreamy baked 192
vegetable rennet 14, 20
vegetables: Cheddar and veggie frittata 144
very naughty mac and cheese 146

walnuts: fig, walnut and honey baked
    Camembert 196
Welsh rarebit 143
Westland 158
whisky, cheese and 209
wine, cheese and 206–7
winter cheeseboard 216–17

yoghurt
    feta 126–9
    yoghurt cheese 190
    yoghurt dip 130

Acknowledgements

Mum and Dad – there are not enough words to describe how thankful I am to both of you. I know I don't show how grateful I am enough, but I really am. You have taught me so much, without you there would be no book and no cheese shop. So, thank you. For everything. I promise I will work hard to make you proud. I have no idea where I would be without your love, guidance and support.

Writing a book is harder than I thought and more rewarding than I could have ever imagined. None of this would have been possible without my incredible boyfriend Bryn. Thank you for supporting me through everything, and especially for encouraging me throughout this experience. I love you.

Cicely Rose, thank you for waking up in the middle of the night to help me prepare for all the shoots, helping me with the cheese shop when I was away writing and being there for me no matter what. You are an amazing sister and friend.

Georgie, thank you for being the most caring, loving brother, who I can always count on for love, support and help.

My completion of this book could not have been accomplished without the support of Jessica. While I was writing this book you have taken the shop in your loving hands and looked after everything. You're fab, thank you so much.

Molly McCarthy you legend! This book was just a little idea over drinks and you made the whole thing happen while running the world from your phone. The queen of PR.

Thank you to James for letting me experiment and cook in your home, especially the kitchen. And for your delicious meals while I was writing.

Thank you to Charlie, Mike, Mel, Tim and Simon at Sunday Brunch for being so supportive and giving me a platform to tell everyone about the wonderful cheeses that are being made all over the world. I love you.

Thank you to all my friends and family who have offered love and support throughout and thank you in advance for buying 10 copies of the book each. Ha ha.

I would like to express my gratitude to the many people who saw me through this book; to all those who provided support, talked things over, read, wrote, offered comments, editing, proofreading and design.

I would like to thank Quarto for enabling me to publish this book. Above all I want to thank Jacqui, Fritha, Sian, Maggie, Joe, Jessica, Melissa, Paileen and the rest of the wonderful team, who supported and encouraged me in spite of all the time it took.

I would like to thank Jamie Orlando Smith for being a wonderful photographer and food stylist, helping me make all the food look amazing.

Thank you to the most amazing inspiring cheesemakers all over the world. You are the reason I love cheese, the craft, the stories and the history. Thank you for sharing your recipes, tips guidance and help – you are amazing! I wish I could feature you all!

If there's one thing that I love as much as the people I mention above, it's you, cheese. Everything about your delicious taste makes me cry tears of joy. You have the perfect textures, tastes and appearance. I love eating you, selling you, talking about you and now I can say I have loved writing about you. I think it's safe to say, you are perfect.

Thank you to the following cheesemakers for supplying photographs:

AFFINEUR WALO, SWITZERLAND
www.affineurwalo.ch/node/159

BELLELAY, SWITZERLAND
www.tetedemoine.ch/en/

BIO HOMBRE, ITALY
www.hombre.it/en/parmesan

BLACKWOODS CHEESE COMPANY, UK
www.blackwoodscheesecompany.co.uk

CAPRIOLE, USA
www.capriolegoatcheese.com

CASA MADAIO, ITALY
www.casamadaio.it

COLSTON BASSETT DAIRY, UK
www.colstonbassettdairy.co.uk

CORNISH GOUDA COMPANY, UK
www.cornishgouda.co.uk

COWS CREAMERY, CANADA
www.cowscreamery.ca

CYPRESS GROVE, USA
www.cypressgrovecheese.com/about-us/dairy.html

FORMATGES CAMPS, SPAIN
www.formatgescamps.com

FROMAGERIE GANOT, FRANCE
www.fermes-brie.fr

FROMAGERIE GRAINDORGE, FRANCE
www.graindorge.fr

JOSEPH PACCARD, FRANCE
Sarl Joseph Paccard & Aftalp
www.reblochon-paccard.fr

KARDITSEL, BELGIUM
www.karditsel.be

KOSTARELOS DAIRY, GREECE
www.kostarelos.gr/en-US/our-cheese-and-dairy.aspx

MEADOW CREEK DAIRY, USA
www.meadowcreekdairy.com

ROQUEFORT PAPILLON, FRANCE
www.roquefort-papillon.com

QUATTRO PORTONI, ITALY
www.quattroportoni.it

QUICKE'S, UK
www.quickes.co.uk

WESTLAND CHEESE, THE NETHERLANDS
www.westlandkaas.nl/en